S0-ESE-435

PRAISE FOR
Lamentations of Nezahualcóyotl

"Stavans enters into the unknown and incredible set of visionary and historical pillars held up by Nezahualcóyotl, the first poet-prince of Mesoamerica. Although cast as 'Lamentations,' here we read the extracts of deep research and 'total' transmission of Neza's poetry, rule and depth of thought, knowledge and vision. Stavans makes sure we take note of Nezahualcóyotl's hidden multidimensional senses: 'I perceive what is secret,' Neza writes. He speaks of 'shape-shifting,' the 'divine voice,' the 'three souls on all human bodies,' the substance of 'words' and the 'Journey to the Underworld.' This is a treasure of unknown powers, paths of awareness, an elastic universe at our hands, voice and mind—gifted by the first poet of the Americas and the first transmitter of his 'Lamentations.' Here is a notebook of cultural and cosmic lightning. A ground-breaker and sky-shaker."

JUAN FELIPE HERRERA,
POET LAUREATE OF THE UNITED STATES, EMERITUS

"Ilan Stavans casts a spell in this remarkable retelling of a king's sorrows. Stripped of all poetic adornments, yet beautifully conveyed, these songs become a moving testimony. Nezahualcóyotl (1402–1472) wants nothing more than a knowledgeable populace, justice and moral civility in a resplendent floral region, a paradise. Yet he harbors revenge against those who killed his father and clashes with rivals in the area called Texcoco, just north of the Aztec capital, Tenochtitlan. A fierce warrior, he assumes his rightful place. He becomes a king, powerful and dressed in colorful robes. Nevertheless, he is like other mortals. He sings, 'I am fallible, I am infinite,' a human contradiction. Here we have geography, cosmology, prophecy, the kingdom of birds and animals, and glimpses of a king filled with doubt. This is Nezahualcóyotl's lament about the brevity of life. An extraordinary work."

GARY SOTO, AUTHOR OF *A FIRE IN MY HANDS*

"The poet king of Texcoco has returned! Ilan Stavans journeys to the pre-Hispanic underworld to recover a lost tradition. If Nezahualcóyotl rebelled against the fugacity of life in an epoch defined by war and human sacrifices, Stavans reverses oblivion to articulate a stunning utopian retrospective for our present. The beauty and sharpness of these poems are such that they allow us to feel the obsidian edge of history. A classic of the fifteenth century reaches us with the divinatory power of dreams."

JUAN VILLORO, AUTHOR OF
HORIZONTAL VERTIGO: A CITY CALLED MEXICO

"How startling to read about a world from so long ago only to recognize the one in which we currently live, beleaguered by war and crises of faith, and facing an uncertain future. Nezahualcóyotl's poems, superbly retold by Ilan Stavans, offer us hard-won wisdom and warnings from a civilization on the brink of breaking. But with the dark days, the poet king assures us, comes the possibility of clarity, restoration, and even redemption. What a gift to receive these enlightening words during our troubled times!"

RIGOBERTO GONZÁLEZ, AUTHOR OF
BUTTERFLY BOY: MEMORIES OF A CHICANO MARIPOSA

LAMENTATIONS OF NEZAHUALCÓYOTL

Lamentations of Nezahualcóyotl

NAHUATL POEMS

Retold by Ilan Stavans

Illustrated by Cuauhtémoc Wetzka

RESTLESS BOOKS
NEW YORK · AMHERST

Copyright © 2025 Ilan Stavans
Illustration Copyright © 2025 Cuauhtémoc Wetzka

All rights reserved.

No part of this book may be reproduced or transmitted without the prior written permission of the publisher.

Restless Books and the R colophon are registered trademarks of Restless Books, Inc.

First Restless Books hardcover edition March 2025

Hardcover ISBN: 9781632063861
Library of Congress Control Number: 2024944170

THE WITTER BYNNER
FOUNDATION FOR POETRY

This book is supported by a generous grant from the Witter Bynner Foundation for Poetry and by the Gary and Carolyn Soto Family Charitable Fund.

Cover and interior illustrations by Cuauhtémoc Wetzka
Cover design by Jonathan Yamakami
Text and interior design by Tetragon, London

Printed in the United States

1 3 5 7 9 10 8 6 4 2

RESTLESS BOOKS
NEW YORK • AMHERST
www.restlessbooks.org

for
IRMA FLORES-MANGES

CONTENTS

PROLOGUE: THE SPELL OF NEZAHUALCÓYOTL   1

1	Ohuaya Ohuaya	13
2	The Place of Knowledge	15
3	Salutations to Motecuhzoma the Elder	31
4	3,702 Words	37
5	Nahualli	41
6	Xochiyaoyotl	45
7	Circular Water	51
8	An Urn, a Spear, a Plumage	61
9	Tico Toco Tocoto	63
10	The Shadow	65
11	Against Fear	67
12	Ode to the Mockingbird	69
13	The Rape of Azcalxochitzin	71
14	Animal Kingdom	75
15	The Dream	81
16	The Slave	83
17	Lord of the With and the By	87
18	The Discovery of Zero	93
19	Ollamalitzli	95
20	Before the Council	101
21	Eight Omens	111
22	Journey to the Underworld	115

NOTES   123

Zan achica ye nican.
Trapped in an ephemeral moment.
Cantares Mexicanos: Songs of the Aztecs (1985)

PROLOGUE

The Spell of Nezahualcóyotl

"My past is everything I failed to be."
Fernando Pessoa, *Livro do Desassossego*

The only Aztec warrior, king, and poet we know by name, Nezahualcóyotl (1402–1472), emblematic Nahuatl philosopher and jurist, a combination of King David's daring and King Solomon's wisdom, who died exactly fifty years before Hernán Cortés's violent taking of the imperial city of Tenochtitlan, might be said to be a Rorschach test.

We have at our disposal a range of historical assessments of him from Spanish chroniclers, some of whom were of mestizo ancestry, from Fernando de Alva Ixtlilxóchitl, author of *Codex Ixtlilxóchitl* (1580–1584), and Hernando Alvarado de Tezozomoc, author of *Crónica Mexicana* (1598), to the authors of *Romances de los señores de la Nueva España*, a sixteenth-century collection of Nahuatl songs compiled by Juan Bautista Pomar, as well as Diego Durán, Toribio de Benavente "Motolinía," Juan de Torquemada, Diego Muñoz Camargo, Bernardino de Sahagún, and others. The composite picture that emerges is of a visionary ruler, religious reformer, poet, mystic, and urban planner of extraordinary reach. Yet all these accounts are based on hearsay: in none is Nezahualcóyotl's own voice available, since neither originals from his own hand nor any accounts from his contemporaries survive. In other words, he is almost entirely fictional.

Nezahualcóyotl's Texcoco—spelled Tetzcoco in Nahuatl—was a city-state northeast of the Aztec capital city of Tenochtitlán. It was founded in the twelfth century on the shores of Lake Texcoco, the largest of the five lakes in the Valley of Mexico. To this day, Texcoco is often described as the Athens of the New World. Nezahualcóyotl's four-decade-plus reign, from 1429 to his death, is the equivalent of its "age of enlightenment." The chroniclers and missionaries I mentioned describe him as a proto-monotheist, a steadfast opponent of human sacrifice, and a champion of education, morality, and critical thought. Given his path, some even perceive him as a variation of Akhenaten, the heretic pharaoh in Egypt whose monotheistic Atenism preceded the Abrahamic religion of the Israelites. And, in his melancholia, some look at him as a type of Hamlet, Shakespeare's "Prince of Denmark," who is defined by self-doubt. Either way, Nezahualcóyotl is an enigma.

All of this, of course, has only contributed to the powerful mythological figure that is Nezahualcóyotl in modern Mexico. There is an entire city-state, Ciudad Nezahualcóyotl, adjacent to the east side of the nation's capital, named after him. His likeness is ubiquitous in statues, T-shirts, coffee mugs, and other paraphernalia. Curiously, unlike other pre-Hispanic icons (Malintzin, Cuitláhuac, Cuauhtémoc, et al.), he wasn't fully Mexica, whom contemporary Mexicans claim as their progenitors. Nezahualcóyotl's name at birth was Acolmiztli. The ancestry of his father, Ixtlilxóchitl Ome Tochtli, is traced to the Acolhua of Texcoco; in contrast, his mother, Matlalcihuatzin, was the sister of Chimalpopoca, king of Tenochtitlan, the largest and most dominant city-state in the Valley of Mexico and the cradle of Aztec civilization.

Nezahualcóyotl's odyssey is extraordinary. After witnessing the assassination of his father by the Tepanec, who were led by Tezozomoc, he was forced from Texcoco into exile in Huexotzinco, at which time he adopted the name Nezahualcóyotl, meaning "hungry coyote." He invested his energy in becoming educated and building allegiances with various monarchs. He returned to Texcoco in 1422 and eventually reclaimed his father's throne with the help of the Huexotzincans. In his quest, he created a broad coalition of city-states in order to defeat the Tepanec. He helped dismantle the Tepanec kingdom by fostering what came to be known as the Triple Alliance, made of three powers: Tenochtitlan, Texcoco, and Tlacopan. His partner in Tenochtitlan was King Motecuhzoma the Elder, a relative of the Aztec emperor who would later face Cortés.

Did Nezahualcóyotl actually promote policies against polytheism during his regime? Was he anti-slavery? The Acolhua, the people of Texcoco, were known to enslave some of their captives, as well as to eat them: like the Aztecs, they were cannibalistic. Is it true that Nezahualcóyotl established a rigid penal system? Did he rape Azcalxóchitzin, the wife of one of his soldiers, and then send that soldier to war in order to have him killed? What was his attitude toward queerness, what for some indigenous communities has come to be known as "two-spirit"? Is it true, as Spanish conquistador Bernal Díaz del Castillo reports observing under Hernán Cortés, that some young indigenous males went about in female clothes? Was Nezahualcóyotl ambivalent about these practices? Might he really have condemned religious rituals connected with human sacrifice? Was his interest in the Nahuatl language authentic? Or are all these facets just strategic "readings" by the newly arrived Spaniards, who were desperate to justify their massive colonial reconfiguration of Tenochtitlan and its surroundings by finding an Aztec ancestor whose beliefs appeared to support their own goals and practices? Even Fernando de Alva Ixtlilxóchitl and Hernando Alvarado de Tezozomoc, who were descendants of crucial Aztec figures and thus might have tried to be somewhat more objective, seem manipulative in their depictions of Nezahualcóyotl.

Nezahualcóyotl's songs appear to have been written not by him and perhaps not even by assigned members of his court. They manifested themselves as oral tradition, after which they were transcribed. Authorship, therefore, is complicated. In his book *Fifteen Poets of the Aztec World* (1992), Aztec scholar Miguel León-Portilla argues in favor of a meticulous procedure to identify Nezahualcóyotl's poetry. First, he says, one needs to establish "the person to whom the song is attributed"—in this case, Nezahualcóyotl. Then,

> one has to find in other independent testimonies reliable information about his or her existence. Related to this is the possibility of adducing testimonies asserting the fame of the same individual as a composer of songs. The third

procedure is a search for eventual independent renditions of one or more of the songs attributed to the same person.

Yet this method doesn't prove that Nezahualcóyotl was a poet himself; it just suggests a connection.

Be that as it may, the songs of Nezahualcóyotl's that have survived are—as with the Bible, Homer, and other oral traditions—a collective endeavor. They raise questions about the mystery of life, engage in dialogue with divine beings, ponder the importance of power, and celebrate the cyclical rhythm of nature. The centrality of Nezahualcóyotl's poetry in Nahuatl culture cannot be overstated. In *Codex Ixtlilxóchitl*, Fernando de Alva Ixtlilxóchitl writes (in Jongsoo Lee's translation):

> In the songs that the king Nezahualcóyotl composed, he clearly said some sentences, in the way of prophecies, which have been fulfilled and seen in our times. These songs are entitled Xompancuícatl, which means "song of spring" and they were sung at the feasts and banquets of the premiere of their large palaces. One song begins like this: Tlacxoconcaquican hani Nezahualcoyotzin, etc., which, translated to our vernacular Spanish according to their own and true sense, means: "listen to what the king

Nezahualcoyotzin says in his lamentations on the calamities and persecutions that his kingdom and territories will suffer."

These are indeed lamentations. With a rich well of biographical information, Nezahualcóyotl's poems are ardent expressions of grief and anguish, some more aesthetically complex than others. They are reminiscent of the biblical moaning of such prophets as Jeremiah and Isaiah. The Texcocan king positions himself as a religious guide, admonishing his people to remain truthful to themselves, not to deviate from the righteous path, to prepare for natural disasters, to be equipped—physically and psychologically—for war, and to learn from mistakes. He sees himself as a prophet capable of uplifting his kingdom in times of trouble. And surely the catastrophes that befell the Aztecs during his reign are minimal compared to what awaited them.

But perhaps it is exactly these complexities—Tlatoani Nezahualcóyotl's persona (in Nahuatl, *tlatoani* means "king")—that cast such a spell on scholars, and they are certainly what makes him appealing to me. When I was growing up in the Mexico of the 1960s (in my childhood, I spent time in Texcoco), Nezahualcóyotl was seen as an antidote to European colonialism, since apparently the poet-king foresaw the collapse of the Aztec empire, articulating it to the Texcocan people.

The twenty-two retellings contained in this volume are based on the Nahuatl songs credited to Nezahualcóyotl and featured in *Cantares Mexicanos*, a sixteenth-century manuscript collection containing ninety-one compositions, which was previously translated from Nahuatl into English by John Bierhorst (1985). For my retellings, I also sought renditions of Nezahualcóyotl's poetry by Samuel G. Brinton, Ángel María Garibay Kintana, and León-Portilla.

My discovery of Nahuatl started with Garibay's *Llave del náhuatl*, which led me to his *Historia de la literatura náhuatl*. I briefly met León-Portilla in Cuernavaca, Mexico, in the mid-1980s—he inspired me to delve into Nahuatl civilization. It goes without saying that my own Nezahualcóyotl is no less imaginary than—and, hopefully, as imaginative as—those early iterations. In "The Place of Knowledge," Nezahualcóyotl recounts his own perilous pilgrimage as a warrior, a ruler, and a dreamer. "Salutations to Motecuhzoma the Elder" is an acknowledgment of his debt to the Aztec emperor as the latter's death neared in 1469. Motecuhzoma the Elder was famous for his leadership in times of natural disasters—frosts, droughts, swarms of locusts. He instigated the Flower War (or "Xochiyaoyotl" in Nahuatl)—fought periodically between the Triple Alliance and antagonistic tribes such as the Mixtec, Ahuilizapan, Cuetlachtlan, and Cosamaloapan—in large part to increase human sacrifices, which he believed would placate the angry gods. He is seen as a hero-god by the Pueblo people in the southwestern United States.

Nezahualcóyotl, the myth, has become an essential component in the construction of modern Mexican identity, which has little to do with Nahuatl language and culture or with the people who speak and practice them. The Nahua—the indigenous people of Mexico, El Salvador, Guatemala, Honduras, Nicaragua, and Costa Rica—have been excluded from the project, the identity, and the ideology of the Mexican nation since its inception. But there are certain details of Nezahualcóyotl's life that we do know to be true. Nezahualcóyotl aspired to protect the Nahuatl language, as is clear in "3,702 Words." He understood water to be an expression of the contradictions in life. He was involved in the theft of Azcalxóchitzin, the wife of poet Cuacuauhtzin. Like King David's summoning of Bathsheba, Nezahualcóyotl's affair brought him shame and ultimate condemnation from his own Council of Wise Men. In "Lord of the With and the By," he offered his theological vision of divinity. His poem "Xochiyaoyotl" is an apology for war in the tradition of Sun Tzu, the Chinese strategist and philosopher of the Eastern Zhou period. And in "Journey to the Underworld," Nezahualcóyotl readied his people for his demise as he contemplated his passage through Mictlan, the Aztec netherworld.

For me, the word *retelling* is synonymous with re-creation. With few exceptions, Nezahualcóyotl speaks directly to the people of Texcoco, frequently using the present tense and referring to himself in the third person. To achieve this, I use a chorus-like voice that repeats lines meant to be attributed to the people as a collective. When pertinent, I juxtapose classical and modern Nahuatl. The use of recognizably Spanish terms in strategic places is deliberate, reversing the polarity of cultural appropriation.

It may interest the modern reader to know that a freshwater fish of the Poeciliidae family, called in Latin *Xiphophorus nezahualcóyotl*, swims the northwestern side of the Pánuco River basin. An emblem of self-reliance, it is said to bring catastrophe to those seeking to catch it.

ILAN STAVANS

LAMENTATIONS OF NEZAHUALCÓYOTL

Ohuaya Ohuaya

In sleep, I enter the realm where nothing is authentic.
My body is made of jade and I have eagle wings.

Ohuaya Ohuaya

Singers, allow my words to reach the dwellers of Texcoco.
Tloque Nahuaque, be magnanimous with our erasure.

Ohuaya Ohuaya

Let us admire the jaguar's smile and the owl's song.
May our ancestors deliver us from darkness.

Ohuaya Ohuaya

Our sight is limited, our character corrupt. We are mortal.
Water grants us life, the sun consumes our aspirations.

Ohuaya Ohuaya

Toque Nahuaque, I am humbled. Renew my song.
Let the fragrant flowers cure our imperfections.

Ohuaya Ohuaya

Awake, I offer you our limitations and our hopes.
May you allow our descendants to flourish across ages.

Ohuaya Ohuaya

The Place of Knowledge

Nitlayocoya, nicnotlamatiya—
I am sad, I am afflicted.

These are the stages of my life:
I am the hungry coyote of the woods.
I was born in the net of spears,
the son of a hunting god.
Much has transpired since those days of innocence.
As proof of my power,
close to my sixty-fourth year on this earth,
I built—
unwearyingly—
a dome
made of the 300 chambers,

only reachable
through measureless caverns,
on the edges of Texcoco.
Alone,
I wonder as I wander
the luscious gardens surrounding it,
and thirst-satiating aqueducts—
a stately pleasure-dome
where I have spent countless days
and nights.
Now,
as I traverse it,
I contemplate
the disjointed fragments
of my life,
building a narrative
where only scenes from the past
pullulate.
And before me,
as I recall the rancorous taste of poison,
I converse
with my dead father,
Tlatoani Ixtlilxóchitl;
my mother Matlalcihuatzin;
my sister Tozquentzin
and brother Cuahtlechauntzin;

the soldiers I fought,
the enemies I made.

Beware! Beware!
Xolotl, our prudent founder,
erected this honorable city
while ignoring omens from our elders.
He disbelieved that
the magnificent vastness
of Lake Texcoco,
the largest of four interconnected lakes
—Lake Zumpango,
Lake Xaltocan,
Lake Xochimilco,
and Lake Chalco—
could ever drown us,
that famine could ever decimate our families,
and thunder could ever flatten our houses.
Nature, in its rage,
confirmed Xolotl's ignorance:
plagues,
earthquakes,
wildfires,
derechos...
But it isn't the gods
whose animosity we fear;

it is us,
the internecine battles
in our hearts
and minds,
the acrimony of our siblings,
the jealousy of our friends,
the greed we share with our enemies.

The ruins of this city
are proof of our misery.
Yet you,
dwellers of Texcoco,
remain undeterred,
no matter how wretched
our human condition.
You
turned ashes into bricks,
allowing Texcoco
to rise again,
granting it splendor,
its design synchronized to Venus's caprices,
our character blossoming into incense-bearing trees
and enfolding spots of greenery,
as you crowned me
your leader,
our rebuilding more sagacious,

our courage admired
from Aztlán to Chichén Itzá.
And even if we fall again
—all things are doomed to erasure—
the lesson of our revival shall endure
in the memory of people
to come.

My birth name is Acolmiztli.
Although I was born Texcocatl,
through education
I became an impostor.
It was forecasted,
in my birth year, 1 Deer,
that I would not be weak and cowardly.
Tepeyólotl, Lord of the Mountains,
announced my command of a vast frontier.
But on a starless night,
when I was fifteen,
the Tepanec killed my father.
I witnessed the scene
concealed in the branches of a barren tree.
I still see the scene
unfolding
in front of my eyes:
his chest open by an obsidian dagger,

a river of blood spilling
splashing his feathered shield,
the earth trembling
as a pool of suffering
marked by concentric circles
registered the fury
announced to the moon
by Huitzilopochtli.

Ixtlilxóchitl's death
brought chaos to our world.
Tezozomoc,
the merciless Tempanec king,
and Maxtla,
his successor,
pursued me,
my father's legitimate heir.
Neighbors admonished:
"Leave your native land, Nezahualcóyotl,
find your vision,
and build a shrine
for Tloque Nahuaque,
so that you might be protected,
and your children
thrive
again in

your home,
granting you a long progeny."
Thus, I escaped,
hiding in forests,
inside caves,
in mountain crevices,
under chinampas,
aware of my fate
as the legitimate leader of Texcoco.
And I hereby narrate my travails,
naïvely,
so that poets imprint them
in codexes and alphabetical texts.

Our one-time foes
are now
our friends
and partners,
since, as is agreed,
two-fifths of the spoils of the Triple Alliance
belong to the Mexica,
another two-fifths belong to us,
the people of Texcoco,
and the remaining fifth belongs to Tlacopan.
Surrounded by quetzals,
with a friend playing the flute

to fend off hyenas,
by foot I fled to Tlaxcala,
my two nephews,
mourning their own father Cihuaquequenotzin,
at my side,
as was my half-brother Tilmatzin.
In the plaza of Texcoco,
where my father had once celebrated
triumphant returns from war,
Tezozomoc made a speech:
"By the pricking of my thumbs,
something wicked must now come
to Nezahualcóyotl,
who looks like an innocent flower
but a serpent is under him."

Beware! Beware!
Concealed,
I listened from a distance,
then escaped to the town of Papalotlan,
the Place of the Butterflies.
One of my servants came along.
As I traveled on his back,
I could see Chiauta,
after which
we passed through Huexotla and Coatlichan.

Tezozomoc's forces
came near us.
To escape,
my servant dressed up with my clothes
and ran like a ravenous tiger.
He was captured
and,
a few days later,
decapitated.
The Tempanec spread rumors:
"Nezahualcóyotl is dead!
Texcoco, bow to the king of Azcapotzalco!"

This act of self-sacrifice
allowed me time to reach Tenochtitlan.
As death roamed around
I hid in the tianquistli,
the soldiers' camps.
Thanks to my Mexica aunts,
who bribed Tezozomoc,
after two years,
on 6 Flint,
I entered Tenochtitlan, where,
through schooling at the Calmecac,
I became a Nahuatl warrior.
I learned not to fear my enemies.

I should have made close studies
of my own family.
My siblings,
through a friendship with Tayatzin,
son of Tezozomoc,
betrayed me.
Once Tezozomoc died,
with his son Tayatzin,
brother of Maxtla,
proclaiming himself ruler of the Tepanec empire
in Azcapotzalco,
he put a bounty on my head.
Chimalpopoca,
the Mexica king of Tenochtitlan,
along with Tlacateotzin of Tlatelolco,
sided with Tayatzin.
But in the year 12 Rabbit,
Maxtla,
driven by his own need for dominance,
raised up in arms,
eager to assassinate Chimalpopoca and Tlacateotzin,
and even his Tayatzin,
fancying their cities,
and,
soon after,
dissolved the Tepanec alliance with the Mexica.

As Itzcoatl, the Mexica king,
successor of Chimalpopoca,
readied to surrender to the Tepanec,
on 1 Flint,
General Tlacalel
rallied the Mexica to defeat the Tepanec.
I joined the effort,
orchestrating one rebellion
after another.
But rumors persisted,
including that, given my age,
I couldn't lead a force
large enough
to conquer Azcapotzalco.
The nobles of Texcoco,
among them my half-sister Tezoquentzin
and my half-brothers Yancuiltzin and Tochpilli,
attempted to kill me
by aligning with Maxtla.
My army,
made of Acolhuacan refugees
from Coatlichan, Huexotla, Texcoco, and Coatepec,
all fleeing the Tepanec–Acolhuacan war,
was resilient.
After persuading relatives in Huexotzinco and Tlaxcala
to fight against the Tepanec,

I joined the Mexica victory,
being crowned,
in Tenochtitlan
on 4 Reed,
Tlatoani of Texcoco
by Itzcoatl and Cuacuauhtlatohuatzin.
However, by then
our precious city was a carcass.
Its one-time glory
had brought Texcoco to its feet.
The good customs and healthy laws
we once lived by
were in decline.
A gift from the gods
was required:
Let your heart be steadfast.

In time,
we, Acolhua,
turned this landscape
into a place of knowledge,
extolling our Toltec ancestry.
My campaigns
have brought us growth.
We have expelled the Chichimecas.
Temples of study abound,

built by slaves we've amassed in war.
A new penal code has been established,
condemning adultery,
robbery,
superstition,
misuse of inherited property,
homicide,
two-spiritedness,
alcohol abuse,
military misconduct,
and sedition,
all of which are punishable
by death in war.
And I have established four councils:
war, government, music, and hacienda.
The first, Tecuihuacalli, takes care of the soldiers;
government oversees the officials, nobles, and commoners;
music, the poets and astrologers;
and hacienda, the tributes from our colonies.
Wealth has allowed us tranquility.

Although a bonanza of pleasure is our reward,
beware, for nothing is eternal.
This pleasure-dome,
its walls and towers girdled round,
and gardens bright with sinuous rills,

will fall,
as all things human do:
my successor,
Huehue Ixtlilxóchitl,
at first will elongate
our entitlements,
yet stumble without care
because fate is fate.
The era of alliances is a mirage.
Siblings will again
raise arms against siblings.
Our own doubts
will foster treason,
making us lose the good we harvested
by fearing to attempt.
Believe me,
disasters loom
whose evil has yet no name.
Therefore,
as you weave a circle around me,
close your eyes with holy dread
and drink the milk of paradise,
for this pleasure-dome
will fade away,
as you,
like me,

become a figment
of things past.
Remember
—no matter how futile
an effort it might be—
the stages of your life.

Oc nellin nemoan—
in truth they live.

Salutations to Motecuhzoma the Elder

NEZAHUALCÓYOTL:

I come from Acolhuacan to celebrate you,
Motecuhzoma the Elder, as your health falters—
tantalilili, papapapa, achala, achala.

CHORUS:

Weep for us, Motecuhzoma the Elder,
whose sagacity climbed mountains and tamed rivers.

NEZAHUALCÓYOTL:

You have faced with courage unutterable disasters:
drought and frost, famine and locust—
tantalilili, papapapa, achala, achala.

CHORUS:

> Weep for us, Motecuhzoma the Elder,
> whose power has built pyramids to the sun and the moon.

NEZAHUALCÓYOTL:

> Our children have been sold into slavery;
> the periods of peace are over—
> tantalilili, papapapa, achala, achala.

CHORUS:

> Weep for us, Motecuhzoma the Elder,
> whose learning opened schools and libraries.

NEZAHUALCÓYOTL:

> You extended your conquest beyond the valley,
> from Oaxaca to the Sea of the Sky—
> tantalilili, papapapa, achala, achala.

CHORUS:

> Weep for us, Motecuhzoma the Elder,
> whose increase of human sacrifices satiated the gods.

NEZAHUALCÓYOTL:

> You subdued the Huastec and Totonac,
> in return for cacao, feathers, and seashells—
> tantalilili, papapapa, achala, achala.

CHORUS:

> Weep for us, Motecuhzoma the Elder,
> whose campaigns subdued the Mixtec, Ahuilizapan,
> > Cuetlachtlan, and Cosamaloapan.

NEZAHUALCÓYOTL:

> In Tenochtitlan, white willows rise over the lakes;
> your ancestors, Huitzilíhuitl and Acamapíchtli,
> > deserve you—
> tantalilili, papapapa, achala, achala.

CHORUS:

> Weep for us, Motecuhzoma the Elder,
> whose fame as a hero-god is known among the Pueblo
> > people.

NEZAHUALCÓYOTL:

> I come from Acolhuacan to celebrate you,
> Motecuhzoma the Elder, as you recover—
> tantalilili, papapapa, achala, achala.

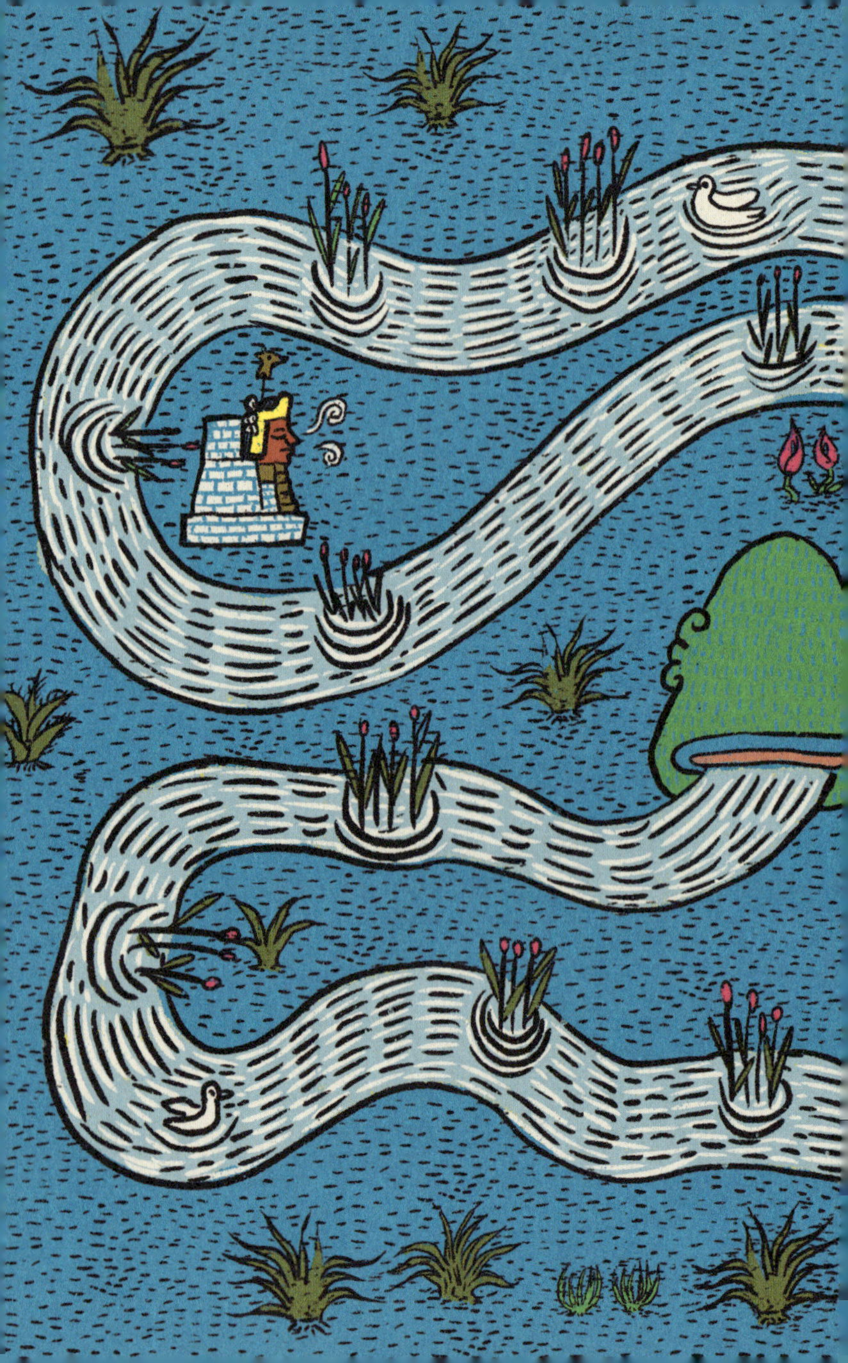

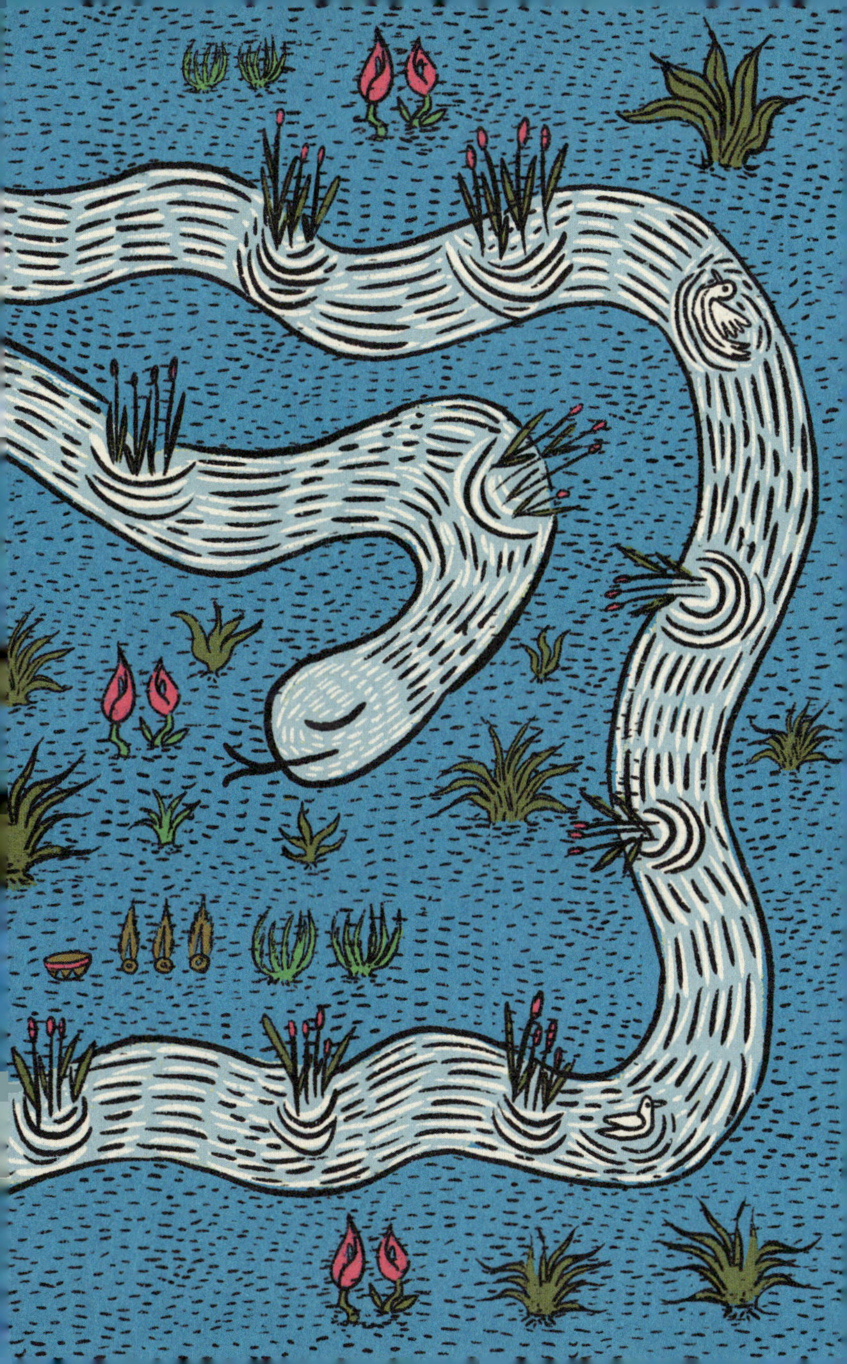

4
3,702 Words

*N**ejamen*: we but not you.
3,702 is the exact number of words in our Nahuatl language.
Caress them,
recognize them,
defend them—
they are ephemeral,
our plumage,
our selves.
   Tzintamalli: buttock;
   acemelle: unpleasant, ugly, ingrate;
      although it might also denote reverence;
   and *xoxocoya*: to invade, to conquer.
Images of sounds, sounds of images.
Each word is an icon
descending from the sky,
conforming a codex

in a screen-fold style.
Words are monkeys,
joking,
sucking agave from the maguey.
Eat them,
drink them,
smell them.
   Xoyacuahuitia: to injure in the face;
   cozcatl: jewelry necklace;
   achiton: a little;
   and *ahuacatl*: testicle of an avocado tree.
Words are rowdy,
like the wind
following no order.
Free, rambunctious, hostile.
Like the quetzal,
they die if unattended.
   Kakawatl: shell seed;
   chilli: spicy tongue;
   and *huixhuixoa*: to shake, to agitate.
I corral them,
I tame them,
I gift them to you.
Call my name:
Nezahualcóyotl,
"hungry coyote."

We are their servants.
   Xocoatl: bitter drink of cacao beans;
   oselotl: mutating fish;
   mococoyaltia: to suffer or fall ill.
They erupt like a volcano,
they corrupt like Chicunauhmictlan,
Lord of the Dead,
invoking the unborn,
in cahoots with Azcapotzalco,
Colhuacan, and Cholula,
knotting the lakes,
dirtying the mountains,
uprooting the plains,
without us and against us.
   Ticitl: medic, healer, magician;
   huapalcalli: wooden home, the mythical house of
      Quetzalcóatl;
   utiliquilia: to bring the road;
   motenehua: to have a name, to be counted;
   monica: survivor;
   nochtli: eatable fruit of the cactus;
   nel: truly;
   tetluzotlaliztli: love.
Where do words come from?
Do they die?
Are there undiscovered words?

Are they misunderstood?
   Nenonotzalli: story;
   mache: maybe;
   ocuic: to take, to grab, to cohabit.
The boundaries of my language
are my end.
To dominate our enemy,
words need control.
Yet 3,702 words control us, too.
   Tejamen: we along with you.

Nahualli

The Nahualli is my shadow:
it follows me,
it protects me,
it appears in my visions.

Since childhood, I received knowledge
from Xochipilli, Prince of Flowers.

The Nahualli is shape-shifting:
it discerns my acts,
it guides my thoughts,
it is my tlamacazqui, my divine voice.

Since I am naïve, I drink ayahuasca
with its black seeds and bluish-hued flowers.

The Nahualli appears as a flaming maguey:
none of us is one,
we are inhabited by animals.
I am a monkey.

Since I am evil, I am broken,
with wings instead of feet.

The Nahualli threatens me:
I am possessed,
I am besotted.
I encounter my shadow.

Since I consume Teonanácatl,
I see light in darkness.

The Nahualli is my conscience:
it feeds me,
it admonishes me,
it departs me.

Since I am gigantic,
I disappear from sight.

The Nahualli is the universe.
I am everybody,

I am nobody,
I am doubt.

Since I am in minuscule,
I am ugly and deranged.

The Nahualli is my conscience:
in rage, I become a bowl,
I become a spear,
I become an axolotl.

I am now your Nahualli.
Zan nic caqui itopyo—
I perceive what is secret.

6
Xochiyaoyotl

War is color—
dahlias, marigolds,
verbena, lilies, and flor de nochebuena
are our companions
as we subdue our enemies;
Xōchipilli,
the god of games,
is gratified
by your vengeance.

Xochiyaoyotl:
war is sustenance—
our singers celebrate you,
almighty Huitzilopochtli,
the left-handed hummingbird,

who wields Xiuhcoatl,
the fire serpent,
as you guide us,
mightily,
to the battlefield.

Xochiyaoyotl:
war is instruction—
festive in his yellow plumes;
you are the sun
always in chase of the moon,
you are vengeance,
admonition,
welcoming blood spilled in sacrifice,
no matter the pain,
to satiate your kindness.

Xochiyaoyotl:
war is ire—
you, youngest and smallest son
of Tonacatecuhtli and Tonacacíhuatl,
brother of Quetzalcóatl, Xipe Totec, and
    Tezcatlipoca,
every fifty-two years
you renew the order to our world,
justifying our existence,

allowing wisdom
to prevail over chaos.

Xochiyaoyotl:
war is attention—
it defeats famine,
lasciviousness,
insurrection,
just as the Flower War
between Huexotzinco, Tlaxcala, and Cholula
taught us. On the battlefield
we test our true worth.

Xochiyaoyotl:
war is strategy—
anticipate the enemy,
allowing him to second-guess you,
in your full senses,
learning to be ubiquitous,
attacking like fire
while following the path of water.
We dance through every move,
stillness symbolizes control.

Xochiyaoyotl:
war is friendship—

as Cuacuauhtzin intones:
by subjugating our opponent
we reinstate harmony.
The sacrifice to slaves might only appease
 Quetzalcóatl
but it is our own sacrifice that instills vision.
For only after total victory is achieved
are we allowed to collect cacao flowers.

Xochiyaoyotl:
war is rigor—
before a confrontation,
all parties selected the Yaotlalli.
Incense and pyre of paper
signaled the beginning of combat.
Our warriors use Atlatl darts,
stones, and Macuahuitl.
The purpose is to subdue others
and punish aberration.

Xochiyaoyotl:
war is mental—
like a hallucination,
it unfolds inside one's head.
It deceives, confounds, befuddles.
The enemy is always inside you.

To defeat him,
we must comprehend our dark side;
to conquer him,
we must defeat our own fears.

7

Circular Water

Yaualiuiatl,
circular water—
imperious,
the earth's nectar,
absorbing heat,
projector and destroyer of power,
blanket of our landscape,
your embracing touch
relief to our callous feet.

Yaualiuiatl,
circular water—
undulating,
your drops bounce,
joyfully,

from waterfalls
to springs
through canals,
lakes,
and oceans,
beyond the Iztaccíhuatl mountain,
to reach the pristine,
heavenly yollotl,
the origin of your being.

Yaualiuiatl,
circular water—
nervous,
it was I,
Nezahualcóyotl,
in partnership with Motecuhzoma,
who first built a garden
in Huaxtepec,
with flowers and tropical trees,
cacao beans,
orchards,
the bearers of fruit.

Yaualiuiatl,
circular water—
convulsive,

to nurture the plants,
we designed a magisterial structure:
a double aqueduct,
serpentine,
a pipe structure
from the lakeshore and the Chapultepec springs
onto the hills of Tetzcotzingo,
running
from north to south,
to satiate the Acolhua,
the dwellers of Texcoco.

Yaualiuiatl,
circular water—
irritable,
I, Nezahualcóyotl, said:
"Water replenishes,
water moves mountains,
water brings hope,
water postpones death,
water renews,
water dreams water."
I said: "Don't bring
the Acolhua,
the dwellers of Texcoco,
to the spout;

bring the spout
to the dwellers of Texcoco."

Yaualiuiatl,
circular water—
undulating,
insatiable,
since all human affairs are doomed,
the aqueduct,
despite its relative longevity,
will not withstand the inclement wind,
brought by Ehecatl,
and the submerging rains,
a sign of Tlaloc,
which, through floods,
shut down Texcoco to one end.
A second, parallel water structure,
made of stone masonry,
with enough space underneath
to allow canoes to travel,
its foundation of sand, lime, and rock,
is hence requested.

Yaualiuiatl,
circular water—
amorphous,

hostile,
no such structures
can replace your gifts,
but enhance them.
However, a chagrined,
remorseful Nezahualcóyotl,
aware that advancement
is also regression,
announces to his people:
Let you be ready,
for it is because of your plenteousness
that the aqueduct,
pleasing Tloque Nahuaque,
contains
our triumph and our doom,
since our enemies,
as they discover the vitality of
Yaualiuiatl,
will also block your supply,
your luxuriant
vitality,
bringing upon us
an abominable outcome.

Yaualiuiatl,
circular water—

impervious,
ominous,
you are birth and obliteration.
We are gullible:
Nezahualcóyotl's aqueduct
is a ploy:
it makes us mighty,
it makes us weak.
Might these two be separated?

Yaualiuiatl,
circular water—
rigidifying,
as you bathe us in freshness,
death stands ready at our doorstep;
it awaits us,
arriving with a smile.
Acolhua,
dwellers of Texcoco,
your children
are grateful for envisioning
another tomorrow.
Forward and backward—
don't be defeated by ambiguity.

Yaualiuiatl,
circular water—
rousing,
your perfection is aspirational.
It is better
to stumble on the road to hope
than not
to hope at all.
Water is generous,
water is treacherous,
water is unanimous.

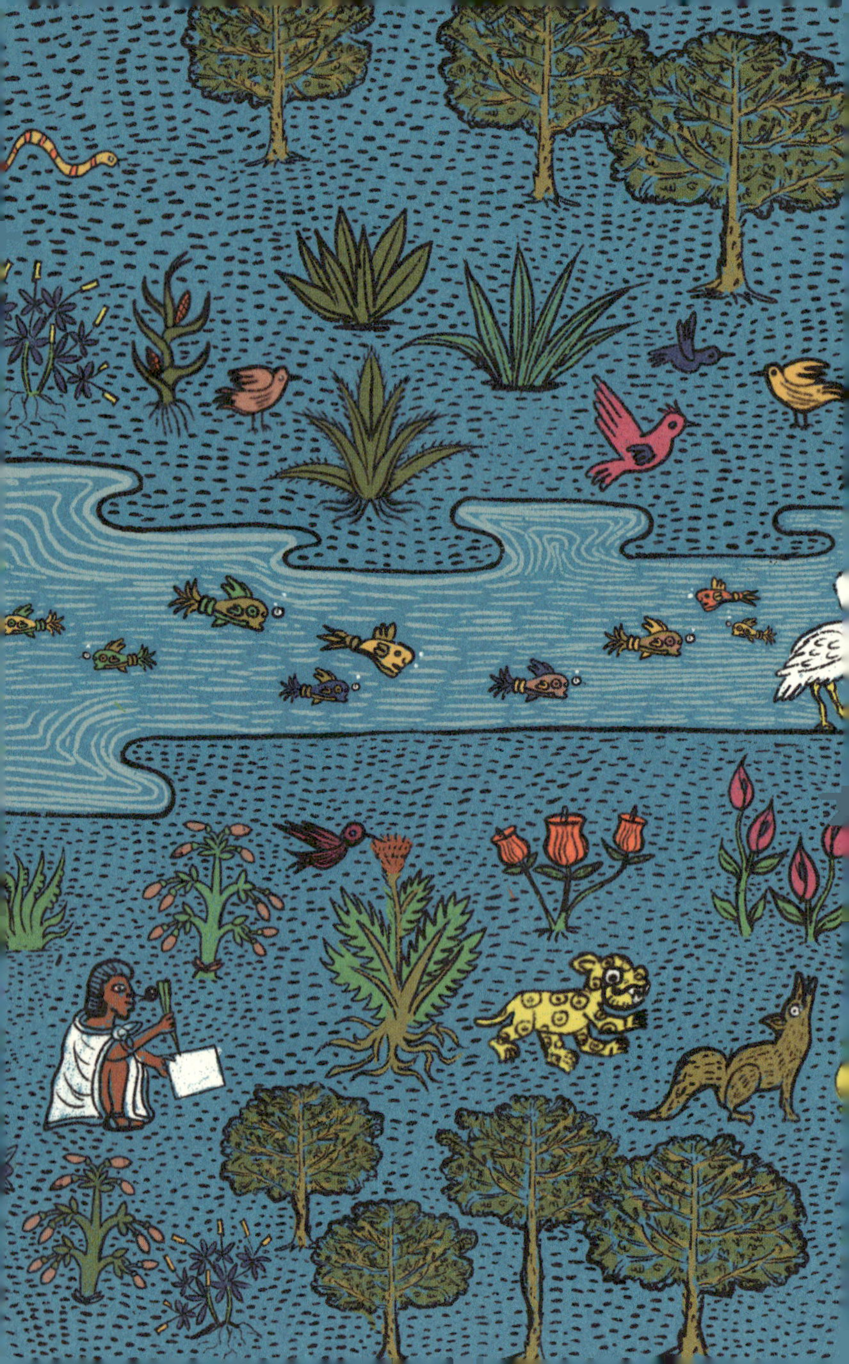

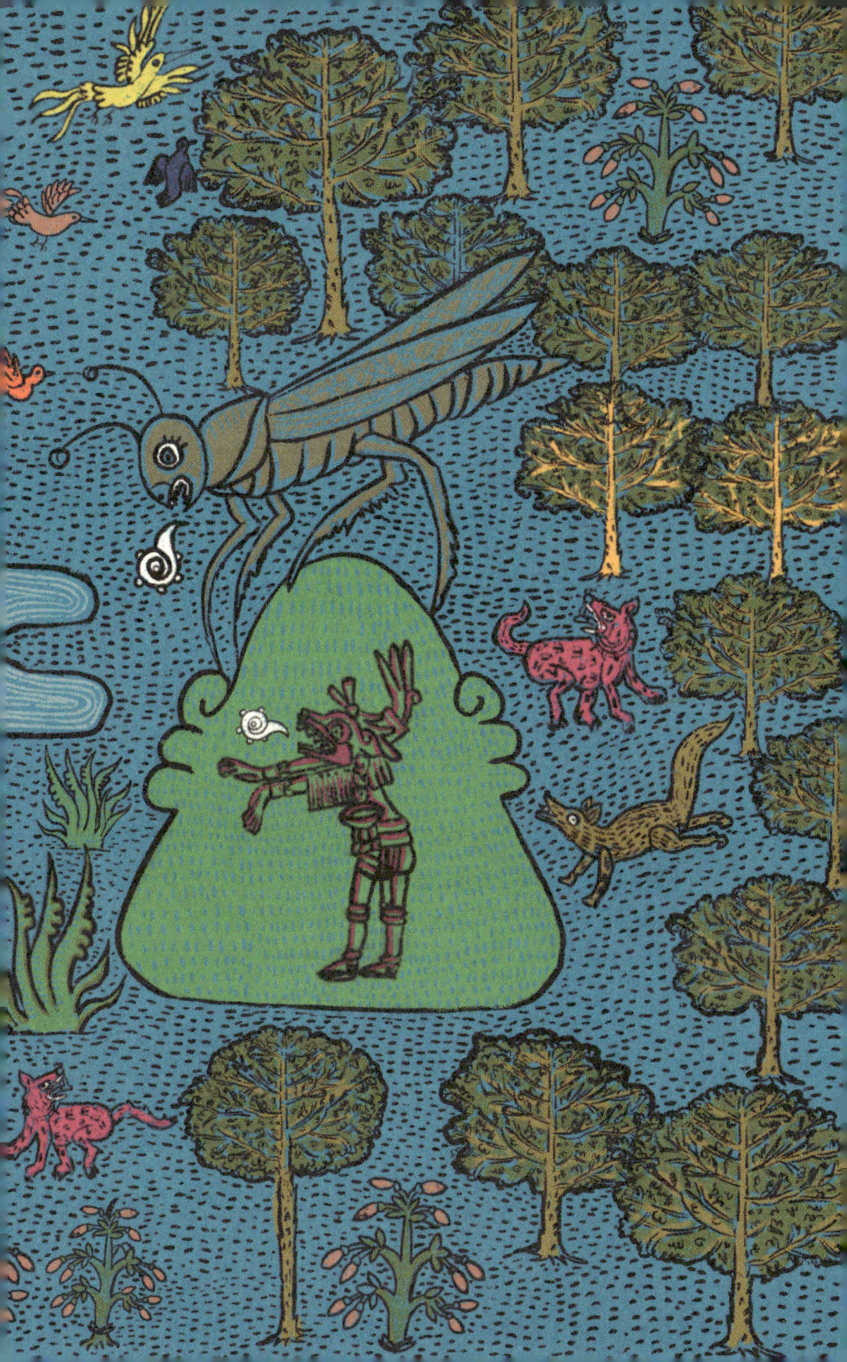

8

An Urn, a Spear, a Plumage

Why do things break?
Life shatters us
and we, fragile creatures,
collapse.
Where do all the pieces go?
Where they belong:
the sea.

An urn, a spear, a plumage.

Death exists within us.
The sea isn't our enemy,
it waits for us.
Let our possessions return
to their original source,

allowing our fibers to sound
like the river.

An urn, a spear, a plumage.

What we have is on loan,
its existence illusory.
We belong to the sea,
its arduous labor of birth,
reconstructs us
until things break again
and again.

Beauty is evanescent
and truth, unremitting.
Don't be fooled by appearances:
though it be jade, it can be broken;
though it be gold, it is crushed;
though it be quetzal feather, it is deceitful.
We pass mindlessly by,
a flash of light bookended by darkness.

An urn, a spear, a plumage.

Tico Toco Tocoto

Earth belongs to no one.
Warriors—I grieve!
Destroyed are the Chiltecans,
weeping are the Tecuantepecans.
The spirit denies us
its song:
Tico Toco Tocoto.

Earth belongs to no one.
Warriors—I grieve!
We Texcocans are humbled.
Drums are resounding
as blood spills into rivers.
We are deaf
as an armadillo:
Tico Toco Tocoto.

Earth belongs to no one.
Warriors—I grieve!
Enslaved are the Xochitecans,
debased are the Amaxtecans.
When we utter the word *silence*
we defile it:
Tico Toco Tocoto.

Grant me reprieve,
Nezahualcóyotl.
You are a resplendent quetzal,
shy,
bewitching the hawk,
the owl,
the toucanet,
the weasel,
the squirrel,
and the kinkajou,
covering our hearts with flowers.
Warriors—we are at your command.
Tico Toco Tocoto.
Earth belongs to no one.
Silence is strength.

10
The Shadow

What has become of Cihuapan?
Happiness is behind the veil that surrounds us.
Ours isn't the best world,
nor the most plentiful.

In another world,
I am not Nezahualcóyotl,
but a nervous bee,
ecstatically pursuing its own shadow.

Where is brave Quantzintecomatzin?
Where do all our ancestors go?
They always accompany us,
resiliently offering counsel.

Where is Conahuatzin?
Ours isn't the best world but the vainest.
In another world,
I am Nezahualcóyotl's shadow.

11

Against Fear

Be strong, Texcocans:
you are now deprived of self,

having arrived in this town of warriors.
I am a Huexotzincan.
I was a slave once, losing my freedom;
I know what bondage is.
You will only recognize power
if you are defenseless.
Your song will not bring you joy.
Flowers won't bring happiness.
Acolhua are coming down
the Tepeyacac causeway.
Tenochcans are surrounded,
Tlatelolcans shed tears.
Wisdom comes from defeat.

Only after you understand your limits
will you conquer fear.

Be strong, Texcocans:
You are now deprived of song.

12

Ode to the Mockingbird

Away, Mockingbird,
immortal bird of four hundred voices,
I confess to you:
my heart is weak with sorrow.
Grant me your murmur,
your graciousness.
Do I go or do I stay?

Away, Mockingbird,
up the hillside,
regale me with the colors of jade
and the intoxicating scent of flowers.
Allow me to fly like you do,
without restrictions,
and love others without restraint.
Do I smile or do I cry?

Away, Mockingbird,
your name is like a bell,
for many a time
I have been half in love with death.
Sing to me, so my ears don't listen in vain.
You were not born for death.
Do I live or do I die?

Away, Mockingbird,
past the meadow,
your murmur has been heard
by others before me, clowns and emperors,
the selfsame song,
and after me, a magic bell in future lands.
Are you mine or just a vision ingratiated with prudence?
Do I love or do I hate?

Away, Mockingbird,
bird of four hundred voices,
over the stream,
I confess to you:
my heart suffers.
Grant me your murmur,
your graciousness.
Do I wake or do I sleep?

13

The Rape of Azcalxóchitzin

Reclaiming my voice,
I, Azcalxóchitzin,
prohibit you, weak tlatoani,
from recounting
the tale of tears
Cuacuauhtzin
left behind,
poet of the Nahua
and lord of Tepechpan.
He himself
summoned his demise
in "Song of Sadness,"
which is addressed to a gathering of friends:
"Where would we go
that we never have to die?"

You, Nezahualcóyotl,
betrayed Cuacuauhtzin,
sending him to his certain death
on the battlefield—
you, who decreed laws against adultery.
He calls you Yoyontzin,
Panting One.

It happened while mourning your brother,
Cuauhtlehuantzin, the Mounting Eagle.
In the house of your nephew Cuacuauhtzin, also
    grieving,
you saw me.
You desired my body.
"Great Tlatoani, Nezahualcóyotl,"
Cuacuauhtzin said,
"when my own father died,
I found this girl in his house,
unclaimed,
modest and with dignity,
ready for marriage.
Her name is Princess Azcalxóchitzin,
meaning Ant Flower."
I am the daughter of your cousin, Temictzin of
    Tenochtitlan.
After giving a large gift to Temictzin,

Cuacuauhtzin announced,
"She is my wife,
although, because of her age,
our marriage isn't consummated."

Seeking, without success, to forget me,
you returned to Texcoco,
where you planned the pleasure-dome.
Before it fell to ruins,
you had hidden in it from Maxtla.

Cuacuauhtzin died in 3 Reed,
in battle against the Tlaxcalans.
Obsessed, out of control,
you had planned Cuacuauhtzin's death.
From what your generals
told me, and from Cuacuauhtzin's war mark,
Wood of the Head Horns,
I knew he was a valiant warrior.
You arranged for him to be sent far and away,
telling him he would become a captain.
I was later told that the soldiers
murmured why Cuacuauhtzin was with them,
since he didn't belong to the battalion.
You made sure he wouldn't survive.
And he didn't.

He was struck down by a poisonous arrow
with peacock feathers.

In the pyramids, the fires burned.
The hearts of prisoners were torn from their breasts.
People chanted in exaltation.
You stayed away from the sacrifice,
asking a messenger to bring me to your palace.
My smile overwhelmed me.
Not until now, having been told by my own daughter,
did I find out you had plotted Cuacuauhtzin's death.
You married me.
You consummated our liaison.

Does guilt overwhelm you?
Adulterers are flattened by a large, heavy stone.
Or else, they are stoned in the tianquistli.
Aren't you one of them?
If the adulterer is killed by their spouse,
the male burned to death
and the female was hanged.
These punishments await.
You shall not preach justice
if you aren't ready
to apply it to yourself.

Animal Kingdom

Chapulín—
wise grasshopper,
you serve Nezahualcóyotl as a guide
in assembling
his miniature kingdom:
animals from everywhere,
as close as Ayotzinapa,
as far as Machu Picchu.

Chapulín—
in the kingdom, Nezahualcóyotl becomes a bird:
a pigeon,
a finch,
a hawk,
a quail,

an ostrich,
an emu,
a booted eagle,
and a hummingbird.
His enormous wings protect the lake.

Chapulín—
in the kingdom, Nezahualcóyotl becomes an animal:
a coyote,
a llama,
a snake,
a deer,
a lizard,
a crocodile,
a rhinoceros,
a leopard,
a rabbit,
a bison,
a buffalo,
and a jaguar.
His sharp tusks defy our enemies.

Chapulín—
in the kingdom, Nezahualcóyotl becomes a fish:
an axolotl,
a rockfish,

and a snapper.
His agile moves defy expectation.

Chapulín—
in the kingdom, Nezahualcóyotl becomes myth:
a Coyametl,
a Tepeyólotl,
and a Zulin.
His dimensions are beyond conception.

How many animals exist?
Do they crossbreed?
Are new ones still created?
Is Texcoco a miniature kingdom?
Is each of us unique?

Chapulín—
wise grasshopper,
bring wind
and fire,
grant me peace
and quiet.
Offer the dwellers of Texcoco
the magic
of seeing
through animal eyes.

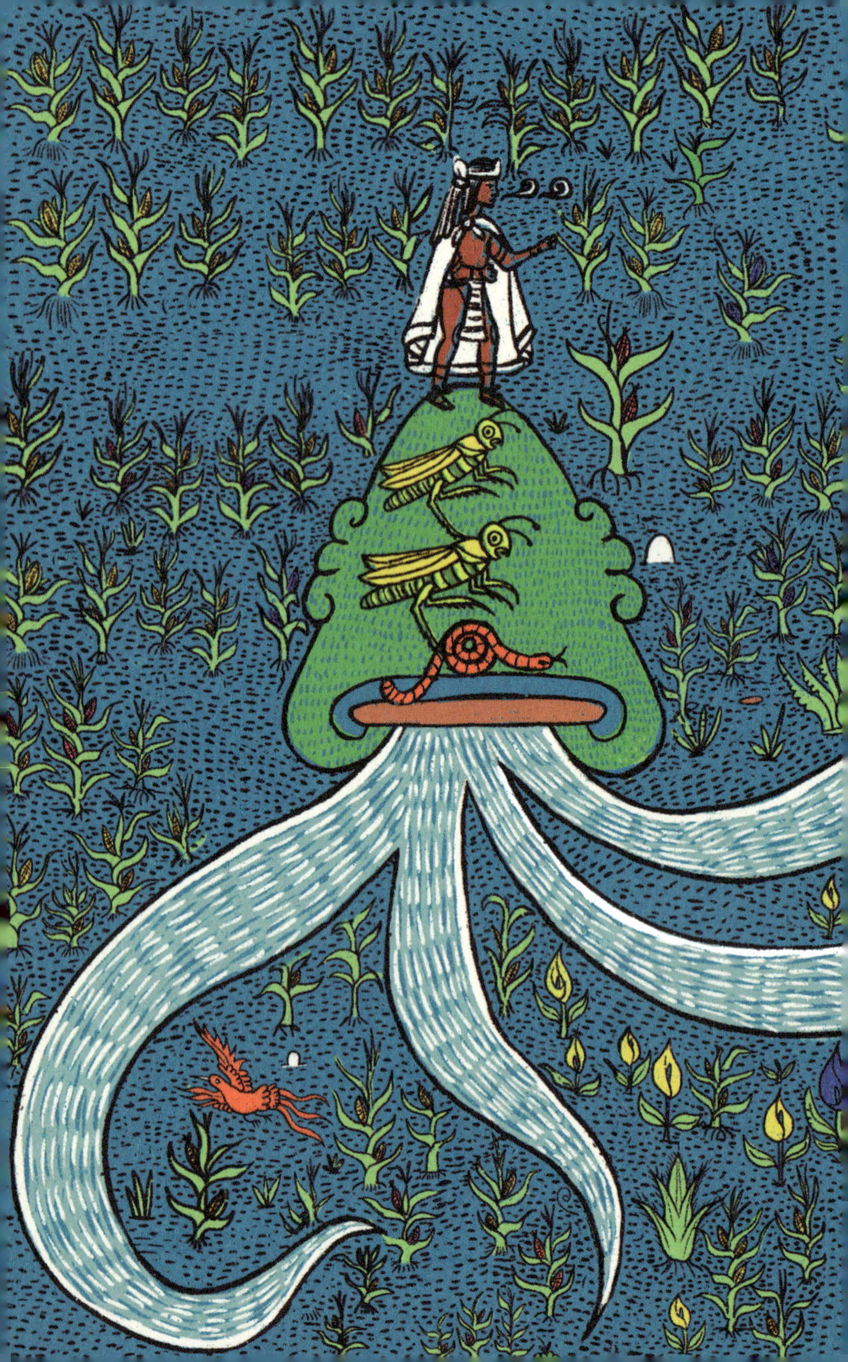

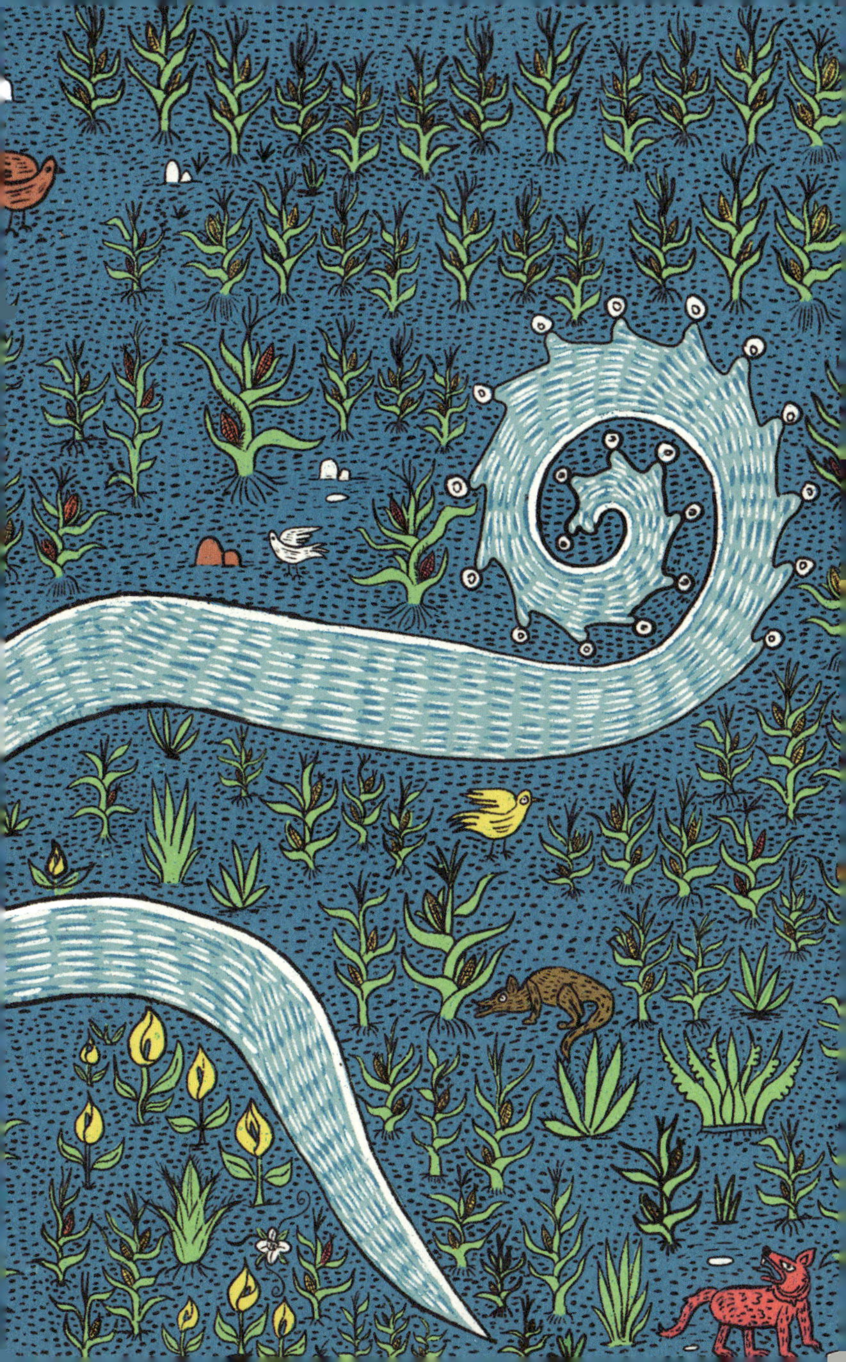

15

The Dream

I dream that the snake devours my eyes;
I see yellow, red, and blue, but not black, green, and white.

I dream the snake enters my mouth;
I taste corn and cacao, but not beans and chiles.

I dream the snake inhabits my ears;
I listen to ocarinas and flutes, but not rattles and drums.

I dream the snake covers my skin;
I feel intense heat, but have blisters and wounds.

I dream the snake flattens my nose;
I smell foul, but not fragrant odors.

I dream the snake rules my mind;
I have my past and future, but not my present.

I dream the snake dreaming me;
I shed tears, but cannot laugh.

16

The Slave

Xilonen is now free;
I am free, too.

Acolhua,
dwellers of Texcoco:
Xilonen became a slave
in the battlefield of the Flower War
after an unpaid debt.
After his capture, he was sent to the lacunae of Cimatan
to work in cacao groves.
Before the war, he had moved military equipment.
And he was a tealtiani,
cleansing slaves before sacrifice.

General Tlacalel
introduced Xilonen to me.

We became friends
in the city of Itzocan,
at the marketplace.
I visited him at the stonehouse,
after the rainfall.
He was always in cuitil,
maguey garments
held by a belt-like strap.

Xilonen said to me:
"Ayec chalchihuitl—
no one shall turn to jade."
He advised me on the fate of slaves,
who, after the battle,
are slain by their owners
and eaten in a banquet.
I myself participate in these feasts.
"Ayac teocuitlatl mocuempaz,"
Xilonen posits,
"no one should become another."

Acolhua,
dwellers of Texcoco:
once, on 4 Atl, I ordered Xilonen
to switch roles with me:
I will now be the slave

and you will be the tlatoani.
Since I want to feel the absence of freedom,
I have accumulated gambling debts.

Indeed, for three days,
I disappeared from Texcoco.
I wasn't recognized by the Council of Wise Men.
I was sold,
I belonged to a rude soldier.

Losing one's freedom
is like dying prematurely.

Acolhua,
dwellers of Texcoco:
I set Xilonen free.
Now wealthy,
he married his owner's wife
after he succumbed to fever.
He owned forty slaves,
but he let them go.
"Ayec mocahuaz—
No one will remain."

His children are free.
When Xilonen dies,

he will be cremated
next to his wife,
along with his former slaves,
twenty women and twenty men.
They shall all assist him in the underworld.

Acolhua,
dwellers of Texcoco:
Xilonen is my teacher—
we are all slaves to slavery.

Lord of the With and the By

Zan te, te yanelli?—
are you real, do you have roots?

This is how I built
the Temple of the Lord of the With and the By,
Owner of Presence and Inwardness,
of Closeness and Proximity.
In the dead of night,
Tepoztecatl,
a magical rabbit
known for frequenting drunken parties,
showed up at my doorstep.
"Nezahualcóyotl,
you're a fool dressed in royal colors,"
she announced.

I listened attentively.
"Why believe in deities sculpted in rock?
And why insist on sacrifices?"
I had no words.
Tepoztecatl continued:
"The Texcoco people descend from Acamapíchtli,
eminent Toltec ruler,
who inaugurated
among his people
the devotion to the Pipitlin,
the god of unknown aspects.
You cherish Acamapíchtli
but betrayed Pipitlin."

I said, "If you are
one of four hundred rabbits
of Centzon Totochtin,
why do you speak evil of Acamapíchtli?"
She replied:
"I don't speak evil.
Instead, I bring you wisdom:
Tloque Nahuaque is neither female nor male;
Tloque Nahuaque is past, present, and future;
Tloque Nahuaque is neither defined nor undefined;
and Tloque Nahuaque is neither finite nor infinite.
Quetzalcóatl the wrathful has long vanished.

To believe in his return is deceitful.
His disappearance is the message:
Quetzalcóatl has mutated.
Quetzalcóatl is Tloque Nahuaque."

I resisted:
"This is dangerous ...
My people will vanish me."
Tepoztecatl answered:
"You shall build
a temple for a divinity
within the boundaries of Texcoco,
not outside,
the Lord of the With and the By,
Owner of Presence and Inwardness,
of Closeness and Proximity:
with the Texcoco people,
by the Texcoco people.
Only after the task
is completed
will your successors say:
'The Texcocatl didn't worship false deities.
They embraced moral action,
searched for light,
and chose the right path.'"

Thus,
six years later,
in 9 Rabbit,
I built a shrine where you,
Acolhua,
dwellers of Texcoco,
pray to abstain from angst.
It is made of four lodgings
which serve as the foundation for a higher tower.
Its nine garrets
representing the nine heavens,
with a tenth
nurtured by abundant stars.
In the interior,
a tenth garret,
covered with gold, stones, and precious feathers,
its ground luxuriating a marble altar made of bronze,
serves as
the Chamber of the Unknown God,
omniscient,
omnipotent,
omnipresent.
Tloque Nahuaque
dreams
all
dreams.

Lord of the With and the By,
Owner of Presence and Inwardness,
of Closeness and Proximity,
you are in us,
around us,
beyond us,
and for us.
You teach us to ask why,
you grant us sustenance to go by.
It is only we who are plagued with doubt.
Don't be displeased,
for our actions are misguided.
Hummingbirds, dogs, and raccoons
are your glory.
Yet only humans stumble,
only humans
become aware of death.

Tloque Nahuaque,
at the beginning
you commanded two deities,
Tonacacíhuatl and Tonacatecuhtli,
to create our world.
They impregnated Omecihuatl,
the feminine source,
from which four demiurges came about:

Tlalauhqui,
Texcatlipoca,
Camaxtle,
and Huitzilopochtli.
You invent the world in the interior of heaven.
I exhort you now:
Grant me favor among my people.
I, a descendant of Acamapíchtli,
the Toltec ruler.
Allow me the courage
to lead by example:
sacrifices don't please any deity.
Only self-sacrifice is rewarded.
Pipitlin inhabits us.
There is nothing in the Chamber of the Unknown God—
and everything.

Zan te, te yanelli?—
are you real, do you have roots?

18

The Discovery of Zero

With a Yucatán emissary,
I have discussed the absence, the shell, the void: zero.
It means plenitude.
In zero, you are full, complete.
You can't reach twenty
—our vigesimal code—
without zero.
The Maya used an empty tortoise-like shell shape to
 depict it.
The xiuhpōhualli,
our 365-day calendar,
is composed of eighteen twenty-day mētztli, months.
Zero is all of them
and none.
In zero, we achieve abundance.
At the end of the year is the nēmontēmi,

a separate, nameless five-day period;
it is when zero represents pregnancy,
breath.
You,
Acolhua,
dwellers of Texcoco,
shall divine
in zero
your destiny:
your quest and its reverse,
your absence.

The Yucatán emissary
announced:
"Nobody lives in poverty.
We are surrounded by precious stones.
Are they perhaps your heart,
Lord of the With and the By?"
While quetzal plumes tear
and jade breaks,
plenitude is found inside us.
As zero
we are born
and
as zero
we die.

19
Ollamalitzli

It's a brutal game—
at ya nech miquitlani?

Outfits are loincloth.
The ball, ollamaloni, is made of rubber—
at ya nech miquitlani?

It's struck by wooden sticks,
racquets and bats—
at ya nech miquitlani?

Players are noble.
They die as ollamaloni hits their faces—
at ya nech miquitlani?

They use kneepads and gloves,
helmets and headdresses—
at ya nech miquitlani?

It is the battle of the sun
against the forces of night—
at ya nech miquitlani?

Games are in stone courts,
leading to human sacrifice—
at ya nech miquitlani?

The young people learn
techniques at the Calmecac—
at ya nech miquitlani?

Huge lumps of raw rubber
are imported to Tenochtitlan—
at ya nech miquitlani?

The trophies are quetzal feathers
offered by the rain deities—
at ya nech miquitlani?

A match might announce
the end of a government—
at ya nech miquitlani?

Ollamalitzli
is the battle of life and death—
at ya nech miquitlani?

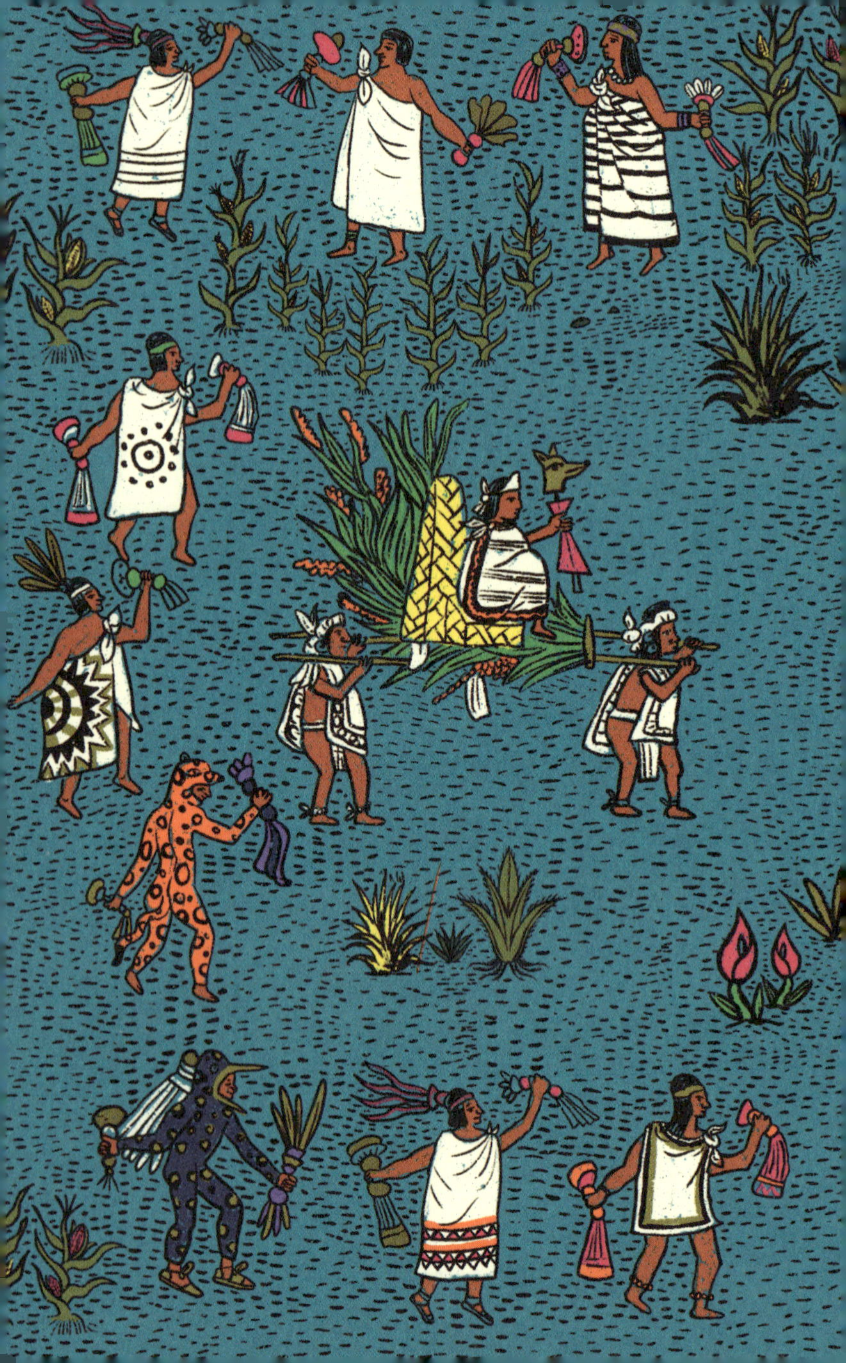

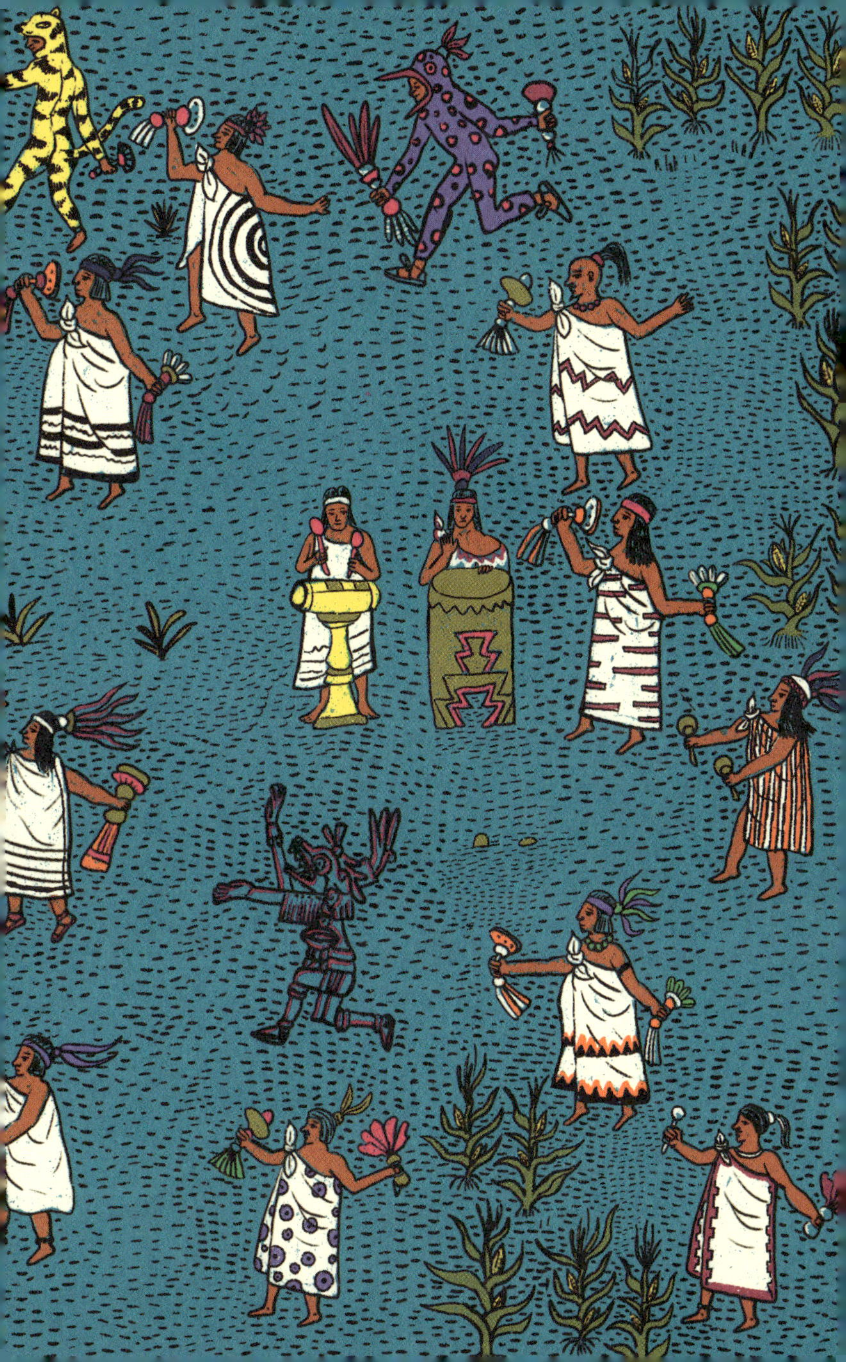

20

Before the Council

COUNCIL OF WISE MEN:

> The dwellers of Texcoco
> have found you flawed,
> Tlatoani Nezahualcóyotl.

NEZAHUALCÓYOTL:

> Summoned by you
> in this portico of the Temple of Humility,
> I am humbled by your queries
> and eager to explain
> the source of my worries.

COUNCIL OF WISE MEN:

> We are the envy of our enemies

and are regaled
with admiration from our friends.

NEZAHUALCÓYOTL:

When young,
I envisioned granting my people
more calibrated knowledge:
I studied the weather cycles,
I built houses for diverse animals,
I studied the movement of stars,
I sought the wisdom of the unknown;
I defied gods
and questioned sacrifice;
I plunder the treasures of my adversaries.
And what did I achieve?

COUNCIL OF WISE MEN:

But in expanding our ambitions,
you have undermined
our beliefs.

NEZAHUALCÓYOTL:

My legacy is in your hands,
the elders of the Calpullis,
and, it is my hope,

in my son Nezahualpilli.
He is made in my image,
from my blood,
in quetzal plumes.
I built a penal code
that embarrassed
criminals,
persuading the dwellers of Texcoco
to choose the right path.

COUNCIL OF WISE MEN:

From the ashes,
your reign has rebuilt
our august Acolhua Altepetl.

NEZAHUALCÓYOTL:

Nature thrives in opposites:
darkness gives place to light,
anger to joy,
knowledge to ignorance,
rain to drought,
and birth to death.
My body
will return to the waterfalls;
it will be part of the soil

and the wrathful Quetzalcóatl,
who forever wears
around his neck the breastplate ehecacozcatl,
a conch shell cut at the cross section,
the spirally volute wind jewel.

COUNCIL OF WISE MEN:

Your view of Tloque Nahuaque
brought us danger.
You defied the rule of Huitzilopochtli
and our other deities.

NEZAHUALCÓYOTL:

I disbelieved all our deities,
attempting to fuse them into a single force,
invisible and indivisible.
I sought to leave an imprint
for the future.
Through writing, those that come after us
will know who we are.
Itzcoatl and Tlacaelel
ordered the burning of painted manuscripts
but I saved them.

COUNCIL OF WISE MEN:

    We wish not one but many.
    Losing our gods will bring only defeat.
    It is our wish for Nezahualpilli
    to distrust your legacy, sending us back
    to the right path.

NEZAHUALCÓYOTL:

    Through you, I suffer
    and spring forth.
    Earth is the place for weeping,
    where breath is exhausted,
    where affliction and awe are known.
    Be chaste and circumspect,
    for when you go astray,
    gossip prevails.
    I no longer wish to safeguard my honor,
    for honor is transient.
    Oh, Tloque Nahuaque,
    I invoke you with flowers.
    Prepare the florid drum
    girded with quetzal feathers,
    interwoven with gilded flowers.

COUNCIL OF WISE MEN:

    We will ask you to abandon Texcoco
    and distance yourself from the Acolhua Altepetl.
    You are a wise poet,
    yet you are imperfect.

NEZAHUALCÓYOTL:

    Your gaze is unmerciful,
    Council of Wise Men.
    Hear my supplication
    to put away your thorns.
    Docility is death.
    True artists are skillful,
    in dialogue with the head and heart.
    Untrue artists mock people,
    labor without care,
    defraud us.
    I am about to embark
    on my perilous last journey.

COUNCIL OF WISE MEN:

    You raped Azcalxóchitzin.
    Power overwhelms
    and rulers are intoxicated by power.
    Their instincts must be tamed.

NEZAHUALCÓYOTL:

> I have lapsed;
> I have been arrogant;
> I have rallied my people to the battlefield;
> I have built alliances based on self-interest.
> Yet I have also rebuilt Texcoco from the ashes,
> erecting temples, gardens, and libraries,
> all designed to erase our enemies.
> Our kingdom was refurbished;
> our language, Nahuatl, acquired a new grammar;
> and our afterlife was surveyed anew.

COUNCIL OF WISE MEN:

> We wish you endurance,
> Tlatoani Nezahualcóyotl.
> Prepare the florid drum,
> girded with quetzal feathers
> interwoven with gilded flowers.

NEZAHUALCÓYOTL:

> Our earth comes from Cipactli,
> the divine crocodile, of indefinite gender,
> always hungry, every joint of its body
> adorned with an extra mouth.
> From Cipactli's hair,

flowers, trees, and plants grow;
from its skin,
valleys, plains, and river sediments;
from its eyes,
caves, wells, and fountains;
from its mouth,
streams, rivers, and lakes;
from its nose,
ranges, mesas, and valleys;
and from its shoulders,
volcanos and mountain ranges.

COUNCIL OF WISE MEN:

You will delight the eagles and jaguars
from the interior of heaven.
In Texcoco, we shall seek a different song.

NEZAHUALCÓYOTL:

Our gods,
summoned by Tloque Nahuaque,
deposited three souls on all human bodies:
Tonalli is located in the fontanel of the skull;
Teyolia, in the heart; and Ihiyotl, the soul of passion,
aggression, and luminous gas, is in the liver.
Tonalli departs the body every time we sleep

and returns when we awake.
Teyolia and Ihiyotl only depart at the moment of death.
Without all three souls, we aren't ourselves.
Grant me strength,
and bid farewell to your tlatoani,
dwellers of Texcoco,
as I intone these lamentations,
not meant for me but you.

COUNCIL OF WISE MEN:

We come to the arms of the luscious tree,
like a florid hummingbird,
in delight of the aroma of dahlias.
We sweeten our lips with them.

NEZAHUALCÓYOTL:

I hear the tentative bells of my tonalli,
anticipating my ultimate freedom.
Time is a delusion.
My three souls shall soon separate,
coalescing in their origin.
Their echo is yours,
Acolhua,
dwellers of Texcoco,
to pass on to the future.

COUNCIL OF WISE MEN:

    Keep a firm heart
    No one will live forever.
    Ayac nican nemiz.

21
Eight Omens

In the year 12 House,
be prepared to stand up,
for eight omens
announce the apocalypse:
the Texcoco people
will be decimated,
erased from the face of the earth.
Keep yourself strong,
hold fast to your beliefs.
These are the visions
with which I was granted:

I. A flying ear of corn,
bleeding in the sky at daybreak;
II. The temple of Huitzilopochtli,
in the sector of Tlacateco,

      ablaze,
its wooden columns accounting for our dying
    deities,
while bells shake maddeningly,
without end,
deafening your ears;

III. Two-headed men in one body—
called Tlacantzolli—
being taken to the Black House,
disappearing once they arrive;

IV. Infected, boiling waves
lashing out of the oceans,
reaching unimaginable heights,
flooding houses,
turning them into aquariums
inhabited by axolotls;

V. Three irate eagles dashing into the house of
    Xiuhtecuhtli,
damaged by a lightning bolt,
amidst a fierce hail rain;

VI. Your thoughts,
suddenly tangled,
untrusted,
lacking a voice,
turned into a source of shame;

VII. A weeping
from a hollering creek,
night after night,
lamenting dead children:
"Come and see the blood on the street,"
   she shrieks,
      "come and see
         the blood on the street,
            come and see
               the blood
                  on the street";

VIII. A disabled white man,
arriving at noon,
bearded,
passing for the kin of Quetzalcóatl,
dressed in a metal suit resembling a crane,
riding an animal resembling a deer,
a mysterious mirror held in his left hand
in which Cinteotl,
the god of corn, earth, and fertility,
is reflected,
looking for treasure,
and behind him
another bearded man,
and another,

      to exhaustion,
      from an undiscovered country,
      speaking mysterious words,
      and leaving in their wake a trail of tears.

This lamentation is a reminder:
we exist in an irreparable solitude.
Time is our enemy.
Yet while the skies might collapse,
our memory is robust.
Ma zan moquetzacan—
face the future with conviction.

Journey to the Underworld

I, Tlatoani Nezahualcóyotl,
intone these lamentations
to the splendorous sound of the huehuetl,
the upright skin drum,
and the teponaztli,
the horizontal log drums,
at the Little Feast of the Dead.

In the year 11 Rabbit,
I request entrance to Mictlan,
the underworld,
if such region is attainable.

Some Tlamatinime,
the people of wisdom,
question its existence.
To me, doubt is the door to perception.

I dream of a place
where death isn't a dream.
Let us go to that house of no tears,
the zone of golden feathers,
the sphere of mystery
ruled by Tloque Nahuaque,
Lord of the With and the By,
Owner of Presence and Inwardness,
of Closeness and Proximity,
also known as Moyocoyatzin,
the entity that invents itself;
let our yollotl, our heart,
find comfort in its uncertainty.
Death—blunt, recurrent, unforgiving—
awaits us all as part of our search.

Acolhua,
dwellers of Texcoco,
decorating the soft edges of Lake Texcoco,
beyond where the eagle might see,
grant me pardon,

nurture me with an infusion of your vitality,
remember me against the lords of oblivion.

Listen attentively,
for these are my "false" memories.
I accumulated them
over decades
and now pass them on to you,
my descendants.
Nothing in them is authentic;
they are false
because, as your ruler,
I am fake.
I am made in your image;
you make me what you want me to be.
The next generation
of dwellers of Texcoco
shall imbue my story
with unforeseen significance.

I am myself a reflection—
a concoction,
a summation.
I, Tlatoani Nezahualcóyotl, wonder:
are we like roots of a tree inside the soil,
not forever on this earth,

only conditionally,
as visitors, as impostors?
Jade breaks apart,
quetzal plumage disintegrates.
Not forever on this earth,
only provisionally,
as a leaf in the wind.

We, Acolhua,
dwellers of Texcoco,
humbly belong
to the empire of Mexihko,
ruled by the magnanimous Axayacatl,
sixth tlatoani of Tenochtitlan
and its magnificent people.
In my bronze skin,
distilling the record of my voyage,
I recognize—infallibly—
that the possessions to be placed
in my tomb
are needless ornaments,
mere enchantments
incapable of appeasing the gods.
I request for them
to be burned
as a return to their origin.

I reject ostentations,
I deny brazenness.

In Mictlan, I shall come across Acuecueyotl,
the skirt of water,
her physical manifestation amorphous,
leaking a seductive fragrance,
a sprawling maguey in lieu of hair.
Although she might display ingratitude,
I will respond with self-effacement.
On behalf of you,
I shall fight the Xelhuas,
giants from the time of the universal deluge;
I shall come before the Tlalcíhuatl Toad,
its head always turned upside down,
and before Xiuhcoatl, the fire serpent,
whose task it is to keep the world in motion.
Finally, I shall come across Itzpapalotl,
the obsidian butterfly,
goddess of Tamoanchan,
which is the paradise inhabited by dead children.

No Texcoco person has ever returned
from the unexplored wilderness of Mictlan,
which proves that the road
to the underworld has countless obstacles.

Xolotl,
the heavenly fire,
is required as a companion.
I have sought
such fire,
I have looked for clues.
There is no philosophical key
to solve the mystery
of anonymity.
We come from oblivion
and to oblivion we shall return.
Mictlan is synonymous with darkness.
To reach it,
the deceased must travel across a mountain range,
followed by a treacherous landscape
where the wind throws flesh-scraping knives,
finally to reach a blood river inhabited by the Ocelotl,
a headless jaguar with an enormous jaw.

Will I find my path
where no one ever does?
Surely not.
I am insignificant.
Lean only on these lamentations,
for they are yours:
find in them the lessons you crave.

No one ever befriends the Lord of the With and the By,
Owner of Presence and Inwardness,
of Closeness and Proximity,
whose secret is found in our flowers,
our song,
our collective vision.
Tloque Nahuaque intoxicates us,
stealing our certitude.
Let our yollotl disengage with the objects surrounding us;
let freedom be granted from our bodily functions.
I am fake.
And after Mictlan, might any of us be granted
a pass to the land where death is nonexistent?

I am fallible.
I am infinite.

NOTES

Although there is much that feels nearsighted, even tendentious, in Miguel León-Portilla's scholarship today, to me *The Broken Spears: The Aztec Account of the Conquest of Mexico* (1962) and *The Aztec Image of Self and Society: An Introduction to Nahua Culture* (1992) were springboards, as were Frances Gillmore's *Flute of the Smoking Mirror: A Portrait of Nezahualcóyotl, Poet-King of the Aztecs* (1949) and Jongsoo Lee's *The Allure of Nezahualcóyotl: Pre-Hispanic History, Religion, and Nahua Poetics* (2008). I depended on Davíd Carrasco's *City of Sacrifice: The Aztec Empire and the Role of Violence in Civilization* (2000) and *The Aztecs: A Very Short Introduction* (2011), Alfredo López Austin's *The Human Body and Ideology: Concepts of the Ancient Nahuas* (1988, two volumes), Katarzyna Mikulska's *El lenguaje enmascarado: Un acercamiento a*

las representaciones gráficas de deidades nahuas (2008), Molly H. Bassett's *The Fate of Earthly Things: Aztec Gods and God-Bodies* (2015), and David Tavárez's *Words and Worlds Turned Around: Indigenous Christianities in Colonial Latin America* (2017).

And I have read, and made ample use of, historical accounts by Fray Toribio de Benavente "Motolinía" (*Historia de los Indios de la Nueva España,* 1536), Fray Bernardino de Sahagún (*Primeros Memoriales*, 1558–1561), Fray Diego Durán (*Historia de los Indios de la Nueva España y Islas de Tierra Firme*, 1579), Fray Diego Muñoz Camargo (*Historia de Tlaxcala*, 1585), and Juan de Torquemada (*Monarquía indiana,* 1615). Plus, I have been sensitive to influences from *lo real maravilloso* in Latin America: Alejo Carpentier ("Journey to the Source"), Jorge Luis Borges ("The Aleph" and "The Circular Ruins"), Julio Cortázar ("Axolotl," "The Night Upside Down," and "Continuity of the Parks"), Carlos Fuentes ("Chac Mool"), and Octavio Paz (*The Labyrinth of Solitude*).

I benefited from my acquaintance with John Sullivan and his organization IDIEZ (the Zacatecas Institute for Teaching and Research in Ethnology), a Mexican nonprofit founded in 2002 that, in association with Universidad Autónoma de Zacatecas and Macehualli Educational Research, provides scholarships to indigenous Nahuatl-speaking college students, training them as teachers and involving them with "Western" scholars in collaborative projects designed to revitalize their language. A conversation with Sullivan on Nahuatl lexicography, specifically on the development of Nahuatl dictionaries, opened new vistas to me.

Much admiration to Cuauhtémoc Wetzka, himself of Nahuatl ancestry, whose florid imagination permeates these pages, serving as a bridge connecting Nezahualcóyotl's legacy and its present incarnations. Subversion has been an integral part of the indigenous population in Mexico since colonial times. Wetzka makes that subversion tangible with an elegant flare. Gracias to three Amherst College student assistants: Rodrigo Aguilera-Croasdaile, Pauline Bissell, Matthew Fisher, and Héloïse Schep. To the staff of Restless Books: Jennifer Alise Drew, Lydia McOscar, and Paulina Ochoa-Figueroa. And to Alex Billington and Alex Middleton of Tetragon, London, for their artistry and careful reading.

◇◇◇◇◇◇◇◇◇◇

1. "Ohuaya Ohuaya": Inspired by "III: Again They Make Music," *Ballads of the Lords of New Spain: The Codex Romances de los señores de la Nueva España*, transcribed and translated from the Nahuatl by John Bierhorst, University of Texas Press, 2010, pp. 178–180; "Poem LV" of *Romances de los señores de la Nueva España*, at the webpage "Aztec Poetry (2): Three

Poems" (2008), translated by John Curl (https://www.mexicolore.co.uk/aztecs/home/aztec-poetry-2-three-poems); and "XLVI: Song of Nezahualcóyotl," *Cantares Mexicanos: Songs of the Aztecs*, edited by John Bierhorst, Stanford University Press, 1985, pp. 225–228. Bierhorst's renditions aren't poetic. Such is the labyrinthine nature of these songs, which were passed down in large part by the Spaniards, that the intricacy of style and complexity of content might be explained but not translated. This is the first of three pieces inspired by "XLVI: Song of Nezahualcóyotl." The other two are "Tico Toco Totoco" and "Journey to the Underworld." I likewise anchored the poem in Shakespeare's *A Midsummer Night's Dream*, Act 3, Scene 2. *Ohuaya* is a Nahuatl term used in songs to express anguish.

2. "The Place of Knowledge": Nezahualcóyotl recounts his life, from his birth in 1402 to his death in 1472. I follow the chronology set by Frances Gillmore in her novelized biography *Flute of the Smoking Mirror: A Portrait of Nezahualcóyotl, Poet-King of the Aztecs*, University of New Mexico Press, 1949. I also based it on "Nitlayocoya," *Nezahualcóyotl: Poesía y pensamiento*, edited by Miguel León-Portilla, Gobierno del Estado de México, 1972, pp. 62–64.

3. "Salutations to Motecuhzoma the Elder": This is an ode to the influential Aztec emperor. Inspired by "LXXIX: Song of Nezahualcóyotl of Acolhuacan Coming to Visit the Elder Montezuma of Mexico When He Was Sick," in John Bierhorst's *Cantares Mexicanos: Songs of the Aztecs*, pp. 367–368.

4. "3,702 Words": This poem meditates on the reach of the Nahuatl language from the perspective of Nezahualcóyotl. The Nahua didn't have a decimal numerical system. For them, 3,702 is the equivalent of 1,001 in Arabic. Inspired by "In ilhuicatl iitec," *Nezahualcóyotl: Poesía y pensamiento*, pp. 82–83. The modern lexical references in Nahuatl are from Ángel María Garibay Kintana's *Llave del náhuatl*, Editorial Porrúa, 1940, and John Sullivan's *Tlahtolxitlauhcayotl*, IDIEZ/Universidad de Varsovia, 2016.

5. "Nahualli": Inspired by "Zan nic caqui itopyo," *Nezahualcóyotl: Poesía y pensamiento*, pp. 68–71. (The phrase itself appears on p. 68.) The Nahua are the indigenous people of Mexico, El Salvador, Guatemala, Honduras, Nicaragua, and Costa Rica. The words *Nahua* and *Nahualli* are the etymological root of *Nagual*, which refers to a human capable of shape-shifting into an animal. See Daniel Garrison Brinton's *Nagualism: A Study in Native-American Folklore and History* (1894). Scholars like Gustavo Correa, in "El espíritu del mal en Guatemala," *Nativism and Syncretism* (1955), believe Nagualism isn't a pre-Hispanic but a contemporary practice. Carlos Castaneda, in *The Teachings of Don Juan* (1968), makes ample use of Nagualismo. My own journey with a Nahualli is narrated in *The Oven: An Anti-Lecture*, University of Massachusetts Press, 2018.

6. "Xochiyaoyotl": Nezahualcóyotl was known as a fierce yet strategic warrior. This poem explores his philosophy of battle. It is reminiscent of Sun Tzu's *The Art of War* (孫子兵法), dating from approximately the fifth century BC.

7. "Circular Water": Among his achievements in urban planning, Nezahualcóyotl built two rounds of aqueducts, from Lake Texcoco to the forest of Chapultepec, amplifying the ways in which water replenished the Aztec population. In doing so, he conceptualized how water was understood in ancient Mexico.

8. "An Urn, a Spear, a Plumage": This poem contains echoes of Pablo Neruda's "Ode to Broken Things," as translated in my book *All the Odes*, Farrar, Straus and Giroux, 2014, pp. 115–117.

9. "Tico Toco Tocoto": This is the second piece inspired by "XLVI: Song of Nezahualcóyotl," in John Bierhorst's *Cantares Mexicanos: Songs of the Aztecs*, pp. 224–228.

10. "The Shadow": Like "Nahualli," this poem is inspired by "Zan nic caqui itopyo," *Nezahualcóyotl: Poesía y pensamiento*, pp. 68–71.

11. "Against Fear": This is a Huastec song inspired by "LXVII: Song of Nezahualpilli When He Went to Take Captives in Huexotzinco," in John Bierhorst's *Cantares Mexicanos: Songs of the Aztecs*, pp. 325–326.

12. "Ode to the Mockingbird": Inspired by "LXXV: Flower Song," in John Bierhorst's *Cantares Mexicanos: Songs of the Aztecs*, pp. 359–360. The poem contains echoes of John Keats' "Ode to a Nightingale" (1819), written in the garden of the Spaniards Inn, Hampstead, London. Nezahualcóyotl was especially fond of the mockingbird.

13. "The Rape of Azcalxóchitzin": This poem is told from the viewpoint of a woman, Azcalxóchitzin, whom Nezahualcóyotl appropriated by sending her husband to battle. The plot recalls the biblical story of Bathsheba, whom King David stole from her husband Uriah the Hittite. I have also sought inspiration in Shakespeare's *The Rape of Lucrece* (1594). *Tianquistli* is the Nahuatl term for market.

14. "Animal Kingdom": Nezahualcóyotl built a zoo in Texcoco, in which he purportedly housed as many as 1,200 different species. The following descriptions are from my book *A Pre-Columbian Bestiary: Fantastic Creatures of Indigenous Latin America*, Penn State University Press, 2020.

From "Coyametl," p. 22:

> A mix between wood-pig and boar, this gregarious beast is capable of jumping over large barriers. In mestizo culture, it is known as a Quapisoti or Jabalí.
>
> Yólotl González Torres, in *Diccionario mitología y religión de Mesoamérica* (Dictionary of Mesoamerican mythology and religion, 1995), claims its principal source of nutrients is knives. The Aztecs also believed it could make corn grow at twice its regular speed.
>
> In the "Legend of Coyametl and the Rooster," structured as a traditional folktale, the Coyametl befriends a seven-year-old boy. After a while, the Coyametl tells the boy he will be granted three wishes. The boy first asks for corn to grow in less than a day. The Coyametl makes the first wish come true. The second wish is that a princess should be sacrificed

in the pyramid of Teotihuacán that same night. Again, the Coyametl grants him the wish. Then the boy, not knowing what to ask for, loses track of how many wishes he has already made. He casually says, "I wish I hadn't wasted the first two wishes. I could have asked to become a rooster." And so the boy ends up a rooster.

Juan Rulfo, author of *El llano en llamas* (*The Plain in Flames*, 1953), talked about the Coyametl to Gabriel García Márquez and Carlos Fuentes when they were adapting his story "El Gallo de Oro" ("The Golden Rooster") for the screen in Mexico in 1964. "It is the opposite of a rooster," Rulfo said.

Hans Gadow, in his *Through Southern Mexico: Being an Account of the Travels of a Naturalist* (1908), writes, "This gregarious beast is easily recognizable by its generally dark reddish-brown colour, whilst the belly, chest, throat, cheeks, and a narrow ring across the snout are white. The usual name of all these creatures is the Spanish-Arabic Jabalí."

From "Tepeyólotl," p. 70:

This is the god of echoes and earthquakes. The word is derived from the Nahuatl words *tepētl* (mountain) and *yōllōtl* (heart or interior). Tepeyólotl is usually depicted as a cross-eyed devil with a swelling and rolling body at the end of which emerges a crown of feathers. Tepeyólotl is believed to have been the inspiration for the pale-skinned humanoid monster with his eyeballs in the palms of his hands in Mexican filmmaker Guillermo del Toro's *El laberinto del fauno* (*Pan's Labyrinth*, 2006).

An echo is a reflection of sound. And an earthquake is the shaking of the surface of the earth that results in an explosion of echoes.

Since time immemorial, Mexico City has suffered from earthquakes. This is because Tepeyólotl, a sibling of Quetzalcóatl, was angry for having been exiled from the divine pantheon. To quiet him, Quetzalcóatl forced him to drink a potion that made him sleep. But the potion was imperfect, and now Tepeyólotl suffers from tremors. Every time he threatens to wake up, the ground in Mexico City shakes, which results in buildings crumbling, fires, death, and loud echoes.

In the earthquake of 1985, witnesses claimed to have seen a cross-eyed devil with a rolling body spit feathers near destruction sites.

In his collection of Yiddish poetry, *Shtot fun palatsn* (*City of Palaces*, 1936), with illustrations by Diego Rivera, Yitzhak (a.k.a. Isaac) Berliner, a Polish immigrant to Mexico, writes to Tepeyólotl (my translation):

> You shake the heart,
> Tepeyólotl,
> deity of tremors and fears,
> returning us
> to the origin
> where death
> reigns supreme.

From "Zulin," p. 93:

> The Zulin is a double bird—or else, a set of birds—that exists by looking at the mirror. Its shape depends on position: one Zulin has a pair of wings, one on the left side and the other on the right. The other Zulin also has a pair of wings, one on the right side and the other on the left. Neither Zulin knows which is which. Everything connected with the Zulin is multiplied by two, then reversed, and finally relocated upside down and inside out.
>
> Japanese novelist Haruki Murakami, in his book *Hard-Boiled Wonderland and the End of the World* (1985), whenever Zulin is mentioned, repeats the word twice. The narrator makes a reference to Zulin Zulin "as an enemy of the INKlings (Inter-Nocturnal Kappas [beings]), sewer-dwelling people who have developed their own culture. They worship a tilapia fish with violent tendencies" (78). Zulin Zulin eats tilapia as a strategy to counterbalance their power.

15. "The Dream": Inspired by "Canto a la huida," *Nezahualcóyotl: Poesía y pensamiento*, p. 46. It is anchored in the ancient Chinese tale about Chuang Tzu, who dreamed he was a butterfly, but when he woke up, he wondered if the butterfly was dreaming he was Chuang Tzu. Included in *Antología de la literatura fantástica*, edited by Jorge Luis Borges, Adolfo Bioy Casares, and Silvina Ocampo, Editorial Sudamericana, 1940, published in English as *The Book of Fantasy*, Viking Penguin, 1988.

16. "The Slave": Inspired by Frances Gillmore's *Flute of the Smoking Mirror: A Portrait of Nezahualcóyotl, Poet-King of the Aztecs*, pp. 121–127. According to the Spanish chroniclers, Aztec civilization was cannibalistic. Economically, it also benefited from the institution of slavery. This poem addresses the feast of owners eating slaves after a battle. Diego Durán, in *Book of the Gods and Rites and the Ancient Calendar*, translated by Fernando Horcasitas and Doris Heyden, University of Oklahoma Press, 1971, pp. 92–93 (as quoted by Jongsoo Lee in *The Allure of Nezahualcóyotl: Pre-Hispanic History, Religion, and Nahua Poetics*, University of New Mexico Press, 2008, p. 159), states:

> All the prisoners and captives of war brought from the towns we have mentioned were sacrificed in this manner, until none were left. After they had been slain and cast down, their owners—those who had captured them—retrieved the bodies. They were carried away, distributed, and eaten, in order to celebrate the feast. There were at least forty or fifty captives, depending upon the skill which the men had shown in seizing and capturing men in war.

The lines "Ayec chalchihuitl," "Ayac teocuitlatl mocuempaz," and "Ayec mocahuaz" come from *Nezahualcóyotl: Poesía y pensamiento*, p. 68.

17. "Lord of the With and the By": This poem wrestles with Nezahualcóyotl's supposed monotheism and his rejection of human sacrifice. Juan Bautista Pomar, in *Romances de los señores de la Nueva España*, writes (quoted by Bierhorst in *Cantares Mexicanos: Songs of the Aztecs*, p. 103):

What certain nobles and lords felt about their idols and gods is that even though they worshiped them and made sacrifices to them, nevertheless they doubted that they really were gods, rather than it was a delusion to believe that some statues of wood and stone, made by human hands, were gods, especially Nezahualcoyotzin, who is the one that vacillated the most, seeking where to obtain the light that would give proof of the true God and creator of all things, and as Our Lord God in his secret judgment did not design to enlighten him. He returned to the worship of his ancestors, and of this there is testimony in many ancient songs that today are known in fragments, for in these there are many honorific names and epithets of God, as in the saying that there was one alone and that this was the maker of the sky and earth, and by himself he supported everything that is made and created, and that he dwelled where he had no rival . . .

18. "The Discovery of Zero": The Mayas implemented the zero in their civilization.

19. "Ollamalitzli": This poem is about the popular ball game practiced by the Aztecs, of which Nezahualcóyotl was an enthusiastic fan. "At ya nech miquitlani?" translates as "Are you perhaps willing to kill me?" It comes from "Canto a la huida," *Nezahualcóyotl: Poesía y pensamiento*, p. 46. The Calmecac was the Aztec school system.

20. "Before the Council": Nezahualcóyotl is known to have established an implacable penal code, although there is controversy about its details. Pomar, in *Romances de los señores de Nueva España*, argues (in Jongsoo Lee's English translation, *The Allure of Nezahualcóyotl: Pre-Hispanic History, Religion, and Nahua Poetics*, p. 120):

> The laws, regulations, good customs, and ways of living were generally kept in all the land ... And it was commonly said that in this city they have the archive of their councils, laws, and ordinances, and that they were taught how to live honestly and politically, not as beasts.

Among the Aztecs, the Calpulli was the neighborhood. It was built based on kinship.

21. "Eight Omens": Nezahualcóyotl discusses the omens announcing the conquest of Tenochtitlan by Hernán Cortés in 1523, in *The Broken Spears: The Aztec Account of the Conquest of Mexico*, Beacon Press, 1962, pp. 3–13. Anchored in Octavio Paz's *The Labyrinth of Solitude*, translated by Lysander Kemp, Grove, 1961. Paz writes:

> Solitude is the profoundest fact of the human condition. Man is the only being who knows he is alone, and the only one who seeks out another. His nature—if that word can be used in reference to man, who has "invented" himself by saying "no" to nature—consists of his longing to realize himself in another. Man is nostalgic and in search for

communion. Therefore, when he is aware of himself he is aware of his lack of another, that is, of his solitude.

22. "Journey to the Underworld": Mictlan is the Aztec underworld. There are obvious connections between this poem and "Xibalba," a section of my retelling of the K'iche' book of origins, *Popol Vuh* (2018). This is the third piece inspired by "XLVI: Song of Nezahualcóyotl," *Cantares Mexicanos: Songs of the Aztecs*, pp. 224–228. They are also influenced by Book 6 of Virgil's *The Aeneid* and Dante's *The Divine Comedy*, voyages to the Roman and Christian underworlds, respectively. The theory of three human souls in the Nahuatl *Weltanschauung*, proposed by Alfredo López Austin, is speculative. It is contested by Justyna Olko and Julia Madajczak in their article "An Animating Principle in Confrontation with Christianity? De(re)constructing the Nahua 'Soul,'" *Ancient Mesoamerica*, 30 (2019), pp. 75–88. Olko and Madajczak argue that the *-yolia* is an indigenous term present in Christian Nahua terminology in the first decades of European contact. They trace the pervasive ways in which colonial interpreters started a long line of misunderstandings.

ILAN STAVANS is the Lewis-Sebring Professor of Humanities, Latin American, and Latino Culture at Amherst College, the publisher of Restless Books, and a consultant to the *Oxford English Dictionary*. His books include *On Borrowed Words*, *Spanglish*, *Dictionary Days*, *The Disappearance*, and *A Critic's Journey*. He has edited *The Norton Anthology of Latino Literature*, the three-volume set *Isaac Bashevis Singer: Collected Stories*, and *The Poetry of Pablo Neruda*, among dozens of other volumes. He is the recipient of numerous awards and honors, including a Guggenheim Fellowship, Chile's Presidential Medal, the International Latino Book Award, and the Jewish Book Award.

CUAUHTÉMOC WETZKA is an illustrator originally from Zongolica, and is recognized for work that gives voice to childhood, the indigenous community, and the richness of native languages. He has illustrated storybooks, posters, illustrations, and cartoons for brands including Google, Apple, Cirque du Soleil's One Drop Foundation, and various publishers. His work has been exhibited in Argentina, Colombia, Guatemala, Spain, France, Estonia, Slovakia, Poland, Taiwan, Canada, Turkey, and the United States.

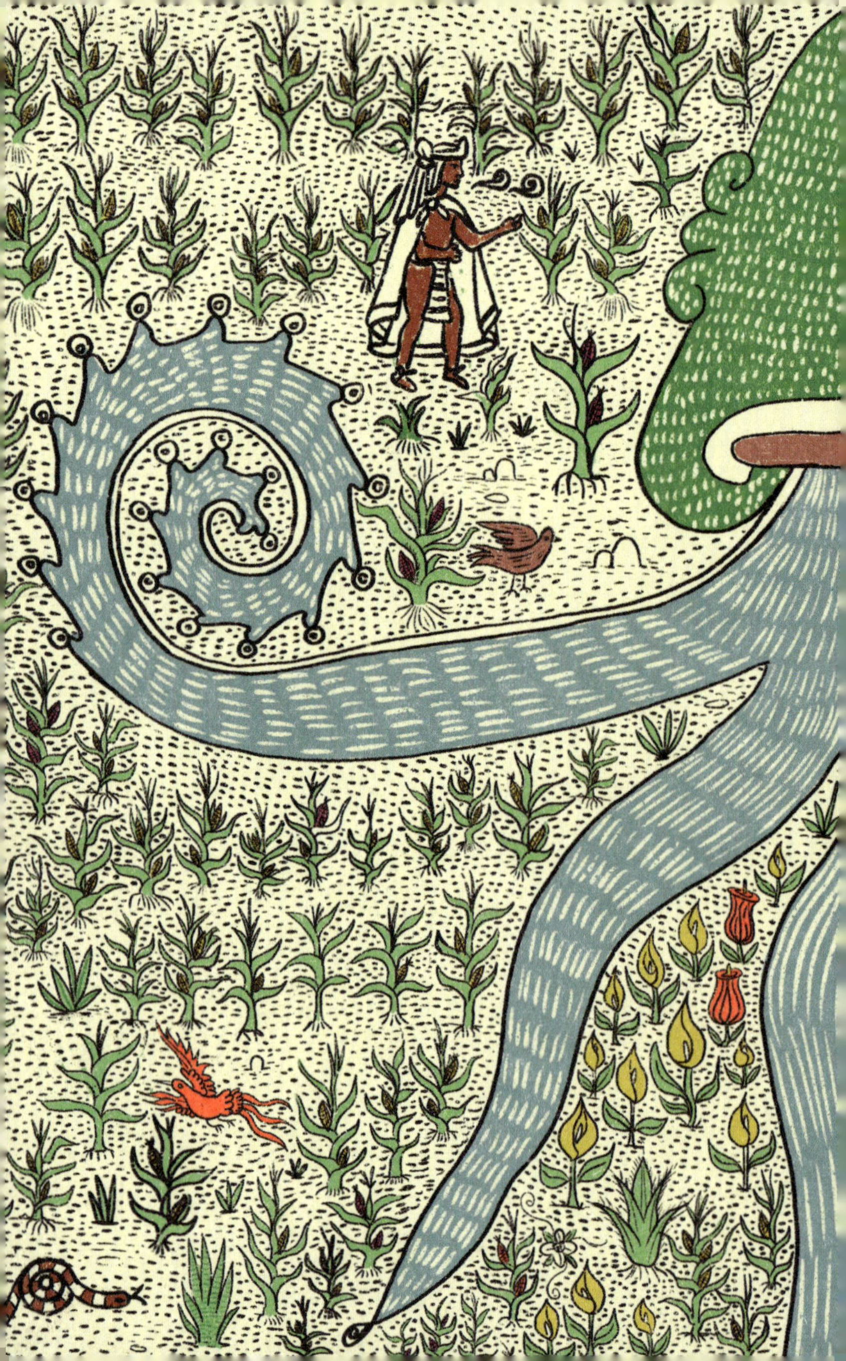